Growing Wealth

Essential Money Lessons from My Garden to Yours

Julie Rains

Hall and Rowe Media, LLC

Published by Hall and Rowe Media, LLC, Winston-Salem, North Carolina.

Library of Congress Control Number: 2022921564

ISBN 978-1-7369605-4-7 (paperback)

ISBN 978-1-7369605-0-9 (e-book)

THIS BOOK IS A personal finance memoir. All information is based on the author's excellent but occasionally flawed memory, including chronology and conversations. The author has changed the names and identifying details of some people and places for privacy purposes.

Dedication

To the patient, kind, unselfish, hopeful, honest,
unpretentious, trusting, persevering,
and joyful people in my life:
Thank you for teaching me what you know.

Contents

Introduction

THIS BOOK IS ABOUT growing wealth, described with metaphors plucked from my garden.

Its explicit purpose is to guide, reassure, and humor you as you strive—and, at times, strategically do nothing—to secure your financial independence. Its secret purpose is to show you how to be kind to others and yourself when learning anything new—growing wealth or growing a garden.

Several years ago, I decided I wanted to learn to garden. While this endeavor might not sound like a massive undertaking to you, it was monumental to me. I likened it to keeping pace with Tour de France cyclists while riding my childhood banana bike with its one gear and coaster brake. Even a tiny cactus known for its hardiness died within a few months under my care.

I knew I needed help. Eventually, I located an instructor who presumed her students possessed no previous knowledge of gardening. She taught me the meaning of *full sun* (the presence of sunlight on a patch of earth for the entire day with no structures or foliage blocking the rays), a term that had been elusive to me for years. She explained that tomatoes require full sun to grow, helping me connect gardening terms with practical applications. After a few seasons, I harvested a batch of homegrown tomatoes. In my corner of the world, store-bought tomatoes are mealy and tasteless. This accomplishment legitimized my gardening efforts.

What I discovered as I pursued knowledge: For others, money is as hard to figure out as gardening is for me. Just as I felt intimidated and confused by gardening, many people fear finances and doing the math—unless they are like me, and they salivate at the prospect of breaking down a financial sales pitch into formulas and a spreadsheet.

While the destination of this book is your financial freedom, the vehicle that takes you there is a collection of stories from my garden and my life. My stories show you how I suffered from and overcame my learning challenges. They also reveal how I discovered and leveraged my strengths, a penchant for numbers and the propensity to interpret words literally, in the pursuit of making astute financial decisions.

I believe our stories inform our perspectives, decisions, and actions. Anyone who gives you advice, whether a licensed advisor, financial coach, friend, boss, or colleague, is influenced by personal experiences. I will not argue that shouldn't be the case. What I will claim is you should know their stories, and more importantly, you should know your own.

My goal is to encourage your growth.

More specifically, here is what you can expect when reading this book: If you are good with money, you will gain encouragement and a structure to help family members and friends become financially free. If you excel at gardening, you will find fresh insights you can apply to growing wealth. Whether your gifts are growing wealth, growing a garden, both, or neither, you will begin to feel comfortable sharing your money stories. In turn, you will strengthen your growing capabilities.

See Unlevel Playing Fields

Before I go further, I want to acknowledge *unlevel playing fields*, including advantages I enjoyed when growing wealth. This notion of inequities materialized for me when I strove to become the top candy seller in my fifth-grade classroom.

After weeks of ranking number one in my class, I was astonished to hear my teacher announce that another classmate had taken my spot. Seemingly out of nowhere, this kid I will call David toppled me. The secret to his success was simple and one we were urged to try: Get our parents to sell for us.

My classmates and I had been charged with raising money to build a fence around my elementary school's playground. The school was new and located in downtown Charlotte, North Carolina, along streets filled with car traffic. The proposed fence would prevent stray balls from bouncing into the streets, students dashing into streets chasing them, and collisions between kids and cars.

I gravitated to this sales campaign as there was not much else for me to do. My fifth-grade classmates lived in neighborhoods scattered across the city, making playdates complicated to arrange. Many of the kids in my neighborhood, including those who lived across the street and two houses south, attended other public schools due to a systemwide assignment process designed to achieve greater diversity.

I became inspired by the candy fundraiser. During the late afternoons and weekends, I knocked on doors, explained the candy sale's purpose, and asked for orders.

The playground fence interested me, but my real motivation came from the prizes. As I recall, if I sold the most candy, I could win a basketball. If the students in my classroom sold the most of all the other classes, we would all attend a professional basketball game featuring the Carolina Cougars, an American Basketball Association team that played at the Charlotte Coliseum.

The prospect of going to a game at the coliseum thrilled me, spurred by basketball fervor in my home state and at home. I had attended

Tar Heels basketball games in that arena—this was during the reign of Dean Smith at the University of North Carolina (UNC)—including an epic matchup between Smith and Adolph Rupp of the University of Kentucky. As you may have deduced, what I lacked in well-roundedness, I made up for in single-mindedness.

For weeks, each time my classmates and I reported our results, I ranked number one in sales. My diligence and lack of anything better to do were paying off.

However, when I heard the news about David's ranking, my heart sank. My parents had repeatedly failed to generate sales for me, previously evidenced by not hawking barbecue ticket sales at my first elementary school and, later, cookies when I was a Girl Scout.

While I traipsed through the neighborhood ringing doorbells, presenting a spiel to those who answered their doors (almost everyone in the 1970s), taking orders, and preparing for a massive delivery, David took a single step. He handed the order form over to his dad, who took it to his office and amassed sales.

Despite my persistence and hard work, I lost my spot as the top seller.

David's efforts, or his dad's, helped our class come in first, so we made it to that Carolina Cougars game at the coliseum.

The outcome made me feel both jubilant and disheartened. It also taught me a lesson I have carried ever since: Life is not fair. Playing fields are not level.

A similar situation emerged with my son's Scout troop many years later. The national organization had created a sophisticated incentive system for its annual fundraiser, designed to inspire each child to sell as much as possible. Once again, a parent swooped in and topped the sales chart with business-related purchases of chocolate bars.

The group's leaders seemed grateful for the income generated by these sales. But they were frustrated because no other kid could compete with that parent. They redesigned the incentive system to reward more than the top seller; in other words, they tried to level the playing field.

As much as this situation annoyed me, I appreciated the recognition of unfairness and the efforts to rectify it.

Back in my fifth-grade classroom, another classmate, whom I will call Rachel, missed school because she lacked shoes. One of Rachel's neighbors, also a classmate, explained the situation to our teacher. She said that Rachel's shoes broke, no extras were available, and her parents needed time to go shopping for a replacement. This happening was in an era when stores closed before dinnertime and neither malls nor big-box stores had appeared in the retail landscape.

Again, the awareness of an unlevel playing field arose within my ten-year-old mind.

Why doesn't Rachel have a spare pair of shoes? Did the shoes break unexpectedly? Did she grow out of them quickly? Doesn't she have an older sibling who could lend her a pair?

The reasons for David's record sales seemed obvious (his dad's intervention); the cause of Rachel's dilemma felt complex and unfamiliar.

I know I've missed seeing areas in which I'm privileged because they're part of my day-to-day experiences, which I think are the same for others until I discover otherwise. Sometimes, I don't know what aspects of my situation to consider. As a child, I focused on what I didn't have—parents who could sell for me—and missed what I did have: a ready supply of neighborhood buyers.

Eventually, I became more aware of my advantages for growing wealth: a God-given talent for math, a brain wired to calculate the financial impact of decisions, a bias for saving, and parents who valued education for their daughters. I also learned of my disadvantages in developing specific skills, as you'll soon discover.

The Learning Curve: Start Here

1

Try to Learn

My first attempt at growing plants failed. I planted seeds for ground cover along a slope in the backyard. My plan was to create a colorful area filled with wildflowers that would cover the bare ground to prevent erosion, just as the seed catalog promised. Six months later, there was no ground cover. I had no idea why nothing had happened and no clue how to fix the problem.

Here is where I stand on learning curves: I do not like them.

Over the years, my lack of success persisted. Houseplants withered. A cactus died. I did not know why. I hadn't yet discovered how to nurture green things or conduct gardening experiments. I decided there were two types of people: those who could grow things and those who could not. I believed I was one of the *nots*.

My failure to solve problems with green things stemmed from the slowness of nature's feedback loops.

Certain disciplines give delayed reactions, a time chasm between actions and consequences, that can stymie progress. For example, green things such as ground cover, garden plants, and grass dawdle in giving me the information needed to correct my course of action. Likewise, financial decisions such as buying and holding an investment, procuring insurance coverage, scrutinizing medical bills, or taking a business risk, may take years to reveal their soundness and results.

A keen ability to see forward and sense probable outcomes can guide you in making decisions, anticipating their impact, and adjusting to achieve goals. I lacked gardening instincts in making the simplest moves. Likewise, you or others you love may fall short with money sensibilities in the same way I had no idea where to sow seeds and how to make them grow and flourish.

I crave quick feedback on what I am doing right and what I am doing wrong so I can make corrections. I strive to become the type of person who can learn from her mistakes, though I'll admit I wasn't sure how that's done—especially in the realm of growing plants.

Several years after the ground cover incident, now a mom, I witnessed a new way of learning—from a child. My observations offered a clue to what I would later understand about my strengths and weaknesses.

One of my sons, Hank, taught me about controlled experiments through his efforts to fix toys and tools as a child. His approach differed from mine.

One day, when he was about six years old, he decided to determine what was wrong with a toy flashlight. He examined the item, asked,

"What's the problem?" and named various design elements that may have affected the flashlight's ability to shine. Then, he experimented with changes to these variables in an organized manner, never repeating the same attempt. He eliminated the possibilities of the source of the problem, one by one.

When I would try to fix or operate something mechanical or electronic, I would rely on past experiences, follow a manual, or test random things and hope for the best, whether repairing a flashlight or figuring out which remote controlled the television.

In the case of the flashlight, my son didn't restore its function that day. Still, he didn't consider his attempts to be failures, merely outcomes that hadn't materialized into a solution.

By watching him as he verbalized and then executed troubleshooting steps, I learned experiments work best when done with logic and forethought. Further, under my son's tutelage, I became comfortable with the concept of refining my knowledge by testing ideas and seeing what worked. Most importantly, I became less afraid of failure.

My son didn't seem bothered when his experiments didn't yield desired results. Perhaps I would be able to adopt a similar outlook, abandoning the psychic baggage I was carrying about my failures and becoming unfettered in my pursuit of knowledge and hands-on skills.

Despite the previous lack of flourishing with the ground cover, house-plants, and cactus, I decided to learn to grow a vegetable garden. This pinnacle of green thumb success seemed out of reach for me alone, so I asked friends for guidance.

Discovering how to enlist help involved another steep learning curve.

2

Ask for Help

Confident I needed direct instruction in starting a garden but unsure where to begin, I asked friends who gardened for help. I believed they might welcome the opportunity to share their knowledge with me. I was wrong.

The responses sounded like this:

"You just do it."

"My husband does most of the gardening. But it's really easy."

"If you have to ask how to garden, then something's wrong. You weren't raised right if you don't know how to grow vegetables. Everybody knows how to do it."

Where did that leave me? I felt shame for lacking green intuition and asking for instruction.

Seeking help seemed to signify mental weakness or laziness. I often felt as if others were looking down on me when I expressed need, whether I should have or not.

The friends and acquaintances I had hoped would be eager to help me and connect over gardening did not offer either guidance or a glimmer of hope that I could learn as an adult. No one invited me over to show me their gardens and explain their planting process. No one mentioned a book, video series, or resource full of valuable insights. No one shared how they became gardeners. Instead, I heard that I should have learned as a child to do this easy thing.

They all seemed to overlook the advantages they enjoyed, the parents who had taught them gardening during their youth, the spouse who prepared the soil, and the hands-on capabilities embedded in their respective DNA.

I had revealed not only my ignorance about gardening but also my inability to teach myself. Instead of being encouraged to improve myself, I felt chastened for my neediness, learning style, and upbringing.

You may have asked for help with money at some point in your life. The responses you received may have been like those I heard when I sought to learn gardening:

"You just do it."

"My husband (or wife) does most of the financial stuff. But it's really easy."

"If you must ask how to handle money, then something's wrong. Your parents didn't teach you what they ought to have about finances. Everyone else knows how, so you should also."

Possibly no one invited you over to discuss finances and show you their savings methods and decision-making spreadsheets or recommended a book that changed the direction of their financial lives. If they offered to help, they might have been more interested in parting you from your money than helping you grow wealth independently.

These friends may have overlooked the advantages they enjoyed, the parents who taught them during their youth, the spouses who set up savings and investment accounts, and their innate abilities to understand financial principles.

Phrasing a plea to elicit a favorable response requires social awareness and the ability to recognize a receptive audience. I had not yet mastered either. People rarely grasped my difficulties with certain types of activities. The advice I received to conquer anything on my want-to-learn list was "Think it through" or "Watch a video." My subsequent, inevitable failures led to self-doubt and helplessness rather than a sense of empowerment.

I could not merely observe a physical task and then complete it on my own, whether starting a car for the first time in my driver's education class in high school or avoiding rocks while kayaking down a river as an adult. I needed step-by-step instructions and a guide to recognizing and interpreting patterns.

For example, when my driver's ed instructor asked me to start the car—the first time I had ever sat in the driver's seat—I asked him what to do. (*Wasn't it his job to tell me?)* In reply, he quizzed me on my previous experience. He asked me if a parent had shown me how to drive along a country road or in my neighborhood or if I might have learned about ignitions while operating a riding lawnmower or tractor. Finally, at my insistence that he, the teacher, teach me, he told me to put the key in the ignition and turn the key to start the engine.

Years later, on a trip down a broad, deep, and calm body of flowing water, a wise friend with expertise in kayaking taught me how to read a river. He showed me how to detect the probable presence of rocks beneath the surface, based on streams of white water. He explained how to choose a path to avoid the rocks and flow smoothly down the river in my kayak. I knew there was a pattern and logic to determining an appropriate course of action in steering my boat. I just couldn't recognize it on my own.

At the time of my gardening pursuit, I was still coming to terms with the specifics of how I might learn practical activities. Later, through persistence and subsequent success with asking experiments, I gained competency in approaching novel experiences. I learned to ask clarifying questions up front and seek verbal instructions for hands-on projects. I became less embarrassed by my lack of intuition for certain subjects, like gardening, even as I grew aware of my math-related strengths. I became more attuned to recognizing people who were willing and able to guide me. But when I sought help with gardening, this way of being hadn't yet happened.

Eventually, my shame retreated—the defeat I felt upon rejection and ridicule for not knowing how to garden as a grown-up. I accepted my learning style as valid, even as others perceived my queries as laziness.

After the early rejections, I resolved not to pester those not interested in offering guidance. The person who might surface as a gardening resource was still a mystery, but my growing desire overcame my embarrassment.

3

Unearth Weaknesses

My friends may have known how to start a garden and sharpen their skills by experimenting with various planting and growing techniques. I did not know what to do first or how to evaluate my results, which was a recurring lack of growth. I needed basic knowledge to begin. I asked for help because I believed direct instruction, not merely learning by doing, held the secret to gardening mastery for me.

I relied on this method for a variety of tasks over the years—starting a car's engine for the first time, resetting a circuit breaker, writing formulas in spreadsheets, baking bread, navigating rivers in a kayak, and pumping up bike tires. I learned to bake cookies only after my older sister informed me that butter should be softened at room temperature rather than melted, a tidbit she shared after learning it herself through a *New York Times* article. On occasion, kind and knowledgeable friends taught me these practical skills. I also took continuing education classes at the community college to gain the information and insights I needed.

My experiences with my sons shone a light on various learning styles.

Hank, the hands-on experimenter, approached learning in a way that was novel to me. His efforts encouraged me to think differently about how I encountered the world, even though I was unsure how to replicate his approach. I did not grasp how differently we learned until my husband and I met with a psychologist for our other son, Sam.

Upon a teacher's recommendation, my husband and I engaged a clinical psychologist to test Sam for his academic abilities. I listened as the psychologist delivered her formal evaluation of this son's approach to learning and experiencing the world.

Sam possessed a rare cognitive profile. He ranked high in verbal intelligence but low in performance intelligence. A ten-point differentiation between the two types of smarts was considered clinically significant; his difference was more than thirty points.

According to the psychologist, Sam exhibited exceptional talents in receiving verbally presented information, performing complex processing, and producing a response based on this information. He had an excellent memory and tended to think literally. Also, he shone in the sphere of numerical thinking and calculations.

This son struggled, however, in the realm of nonverbal reasoning. He experienced difficulties in interpreting social cues and complying with social norms, recognizing patterns and applying this knowledge to making decisions, noticing visual details, and navigating novel situations.

My subsequent research indicated a possible name for this learning style: nonverbal learning disorder or NVLD. My son's strengths and weaknesses (and mine) aligned with the characteristics of this style, except for our intuition with numbers.

In practical terms, my son excelled when learning about the world through words and numbers. He had difficulty learning through observation and applying what many call "common sense."

None of this information surprised me. I perceived the world as he did.

What floored me: My son's way of being was considered unusual. Less than 1 percent of children shared this cognitive profile.

Upon hearing this news, my world was upended. This revelation threw my former way of understanding people and their intellects into disarray, like a carefully constructed and completed jigsaw puzzle tossed in the air. But then, in a flash, I embraced a fresh way of seeing my son, myself, and other people as the puzzle pieces fell into a new arrangement.

Until this moment, I believed people were either thinkers or doers. The few who excelled at both were surgeons, jet pilots, and inventors. I embraced this delineation because no one I knew seemed to excel at applying intellect to hands-on tasks. Then it dawned on me: I and perhaps several family members did not do both well. That didn't mean it couldn't be done, just that I hadn't witnessed or recognized this combination of talents in others.

I scanned my memory of family members' professions to confirm or invalidate this new information. My knowledge of family history reached back generations. Among us, there were no extraordinary farmers of whom I was aware. No family members stood out as engineers, mechanics, architects, or plumbers. There were also no air traffic controllers or radiologists, professions the psychologist suggested would be out of Sam's reach due to his lack of visual-spatial abilities.

People like us concentrated more on thinking and less on doing. Family members benefited professionally and personally from strengths in language, analytical thinking, and math. In specific disciplines, such as finance and foreign languages, we, the fewer than 1 percent, excelled.

For example, I graduated in the top 5 percent of my high school class and earned a bachelor's degree in business and finance from a top-ranked state university. Academic success as a student and being good with numbers and words as an adult, however, masked my inability to learn through observation and, well, do things.

In my family, hands-on tasks, such as repairing engines, constructing things with power tools, maintaining a well-groomed yard, or decorating elegantly, tended to be hired out or ignored.

The psychologist's words revealed my error in extrapolating my brain's wiring to the rest of the world. I contemplated this finding as I then saw Hank, who pressed buttons to see what would happen, who rendered the front door's deadbolt useless while playing, who thrived on increasingly complex building sets, as the "normal" one.

At last, I had unearthed a verifiable, documented explanation for why Sam and I struggled with doing things like gardening and absorbing knowledge through observation. We did not learn how other people did.

He and I needed explicit, detailed, and, often, repeated instruction to learn certain skills. I couldn't figure out gardening on my own, so I asked for help.

4

Recognize Strengths

Growing a garden required capabilities beyond my natural ones. Growing wealth, however, benefited from my strengths, which were honed as I relied more and more on analyzing the finer points of a financial deal and doing the math, not reading the room. I mined for meaning in spreadsheet models and financial contracts, not because I aimed to develop these talents but because I had to use them again and again.

There are two schools of thought about dealing with strengths and weaknesses to achieve goals. The first argues that you must capitalize on your strengths and outsource tasks associated with any deficits. The second suggests strengthening your weaknesses so they don't diminish your efforts and thwart your triumphs. I don't know which is a better strategy. I do know, however, that it's helpful to be aware of your strengths and weaknesses.

During my school years, my learning style didn't fall into then-recognized categories. It would be more than ten years after my college graduation when the term "neurodiversity" was coined. Despite the lack of nomenclature for my learning style, as I grew up, I began to grasp my strengths and weaknesses.

By the time I was in sixth grade, I would skip questions with geometric shapes on aptitude tests, telling myself I wouldn't make a good architect anyway. In junior high, my math scores placed me in higher-level classes for this subject, even though I was not considered "gifted" academically overall. And I got noticed in high school.

When I was a sophomore, my English teacher observed a conversation with a classmate about sentence diagramming. While I was wondering why the person sitting next to me seemed slow to grasp this rule-based exercise, my teacher realized I did not belong in her classroom. She arranged my placement in a more advanced class. This transition, though helpful, was awkward in its timing—I ended up missing lessons in Shakespeare and classic literature along with the instruction I needed to overcome the pitfalls of my unusual way of seeing the world.

To earn high grades in English throughout high school and college, I read assigned books and then scoured CliffsNotes® to decode symbolism and storylines. Yet again, my strengths in thinking concretely and receiving information masked my weaknesses in understanding abstractions like metaphors and story arcs.

Before my son's session with the psychologist, cultivating my strengths meant ignoring my weaknesses. Soon after, I discovered a better approach: seek help from those willing to teach me what I can't learn independently.

You may have been lauded for your strengths. You may have relied on them to land a job or run a business that generates loads of cash. Meanwhile, your unidentified weaknesses may have impeded you from achieving financial freedom or other goals.

For example, you may thrive in your career and earn a high salary because of your industry knowledge, excellent communication skills, and keen ability to advocate for yourself and your team. But though you may figure your income will exceed your expenses, eventually, maintaining a lifestyle that matches your image can be costly. Further, you may believe you don't have the acumen or inclination to amass investments, even though you're probably aware of the need to build something for yourself outside of your employment.

In another scenario, your visual strengths in envisioning future possibilities may enable you to create art, design outdoor and indoor spaces, and plan communities. Drawing on your instincts surrounding elegance and function plus the ability to see potential well before everyone else, you may know where and when to buy artwork, creative works, and real estate that rockets in price. But it's possible you haven't conquered your fear of math in calculating the costs of construction, development, and ever-increasing selling and administrative expenses. So, the properties you trade don't deliver much in profits.

My point isn't that you're doomed if your strengths aren't the same as mine. It's that naming your strengths and knowing your weaknesses can improve your well-being and your finances.

Though imagery escaped me, understanding the concrete in terms of numbers came naturally. Concepts such as compound growth and time values of money taught first by an elementary school teacher and then by my college professors gave me what I needed to make decisions affecting my family's finances.

What I've come to understand is that whether your strengths lie in math, biology, English, recess, or all of these, you can leverage your talents and overcome any shortcomings to master a learning curve. Your path, however, may look different than mine. An excellent teacher can smooth the way.

5

Set a Goal

WHAT MOTIVATED ME TO pursue the hands-on skill of gardening was murky. It was clear, though, that I wanted to learn to grow a home vegetable garden and I needed help.

Was I fascinated with my friends' gardens and their growing abilities? Did I want ready access to fresh vegetables, herbs, and fruit? Would a garden free me from the tyranny of produce shopping? Could I overcome my past and learn to do something that required earthy knowledge, patience, and nurturing insight? Yes, I wanted all of these.

Undeterred by previous failures in both growing green things and asking for help, I added *learn to garden* to my list of goals for the new year.

Soon afterward, an offer arrived via email: a locally taught gardening course at a special price. The offer came from an instructor who was a gardening expert and entrepreneur. She promised to provide hands-on instruction in vegetable gardening and more. I snagged the deal and signed up for a class.

Both digital deals and independent gardening teachers were new to me. Trying this unconventional approach seemed worth the price of a class and an afternoon devoted to learning.

How can you learn about money? Consider setting a goal to deal with one aspect of your finances, just as I tackled vegetable gardening, rather than growing all kinds of green things at the start. For example, focus on checking accounts or renter's insurance or your employer's retirement plan.

Locating useful resources can be simpler if you're dealing with a well-defined topic.

If you believe you'd benefit from direct instruction, take your time to find the right person. Look for someone who is knowledgeable, experienced, and successful; familiar with common mistakes and misperceptions; and free of a hidden agenda to sell you peripheral products and services. Possibilities include a friend, family member, community college instructor, or independent guide like the person who helped me.

Within a few months of setting my learn-to-garden goal and signing up for the class, I met the teacher who would help me redefine my ability to do things.

6

Find the Right Guide

What made me choose this instructor was her willingness to teach me. My friends did not want to help me, but she did. When I received her "Learn to Garden" offer soon after setting my goal, I believed providence had connected us. I decided to devour any morsel of insight she might suggest, and if none appeared, well, I would have spent a pleasant afternoon away from my office.

On the day of the class, I drove an hour to reach her home and place of business, situated on several acres overlooking a lake. Her property included an outbuilding that doubled as a teaching studio and tool shed.

Upon my arrival, she greeted me, welcomed my fellow students, and invited us into her home. The students numbered about ten to fifteen. Nearly half seemed to be devotees of her gardening sessions, and the other half were newbies like me, curious and eager to see what might happen next.

Inside, she showed us highlights of her house, including floor-to-ceiling windows overlooking the waterfront. Next, she offered us beverages, part of the package deal. I began to feel like a guest, not a paying student.

My newfound gardening teacher started the instructional part of the program amidst her green space outside. She showed us her gardening handiwork, consisting of vegetable and herb gardens as well as formal landscaping with trees, grasses, and shrubbery. While I had signed up to learn to grow a vegetable garden, she awakened me to growing possibilities.

As we gathered and walked the grounds, a few of her regulars posed questions to solve their gardening mysteries, such as how to deter deer from feasting on still-growing vegetables.

She responded with phrases like, "Well, you've probably been told to [fill in the blank with traditional advice], but what really works is [a simple, practical solution]."

Her answers endeared me to her and gave me hope I could learn to separate gardening myths from truths. Clearly, she recognized that budding gardeners failed even when we followed instructions. She knew that incorrect information and inappropriate guidance littered the realm of garden problem solving. Any residual shame I was carrying with me evaporated in the presence of this compassionate teacher.

For the classroom instruction, she took us to the teaching studio. There she distributed reference materials and imparted her knowledge in the content portion of the lesson. What struck me about this session was its simplicity and clarity. In approximately one hour, my instructor revealed the secret to successful gardening in the form of three ingredients: good soil, sunlight, and water.

"Without good soil," she said, "nothing else matters."

No amount of soil additives, fancy equipment, or special techniques could replace good dirt.

The teacher revealed the definition of full sun, a term that had bewildered me. She explained how water jump-started the mystery and miracle of seed germination.

Equipped with these basics, I believed I could succeed.

Recalling this session, I see the secret to my teacher's effectiveness, beyond her willingness to help. She gave me what I needed to know using words, concrete ones, suitable to my learning level and style. I imagine I could have spent hours watching someone tend a garden without being able to infer these growing principles.

This lesson set in motion my transformation from a novice, stuck in a cycle of repeating mistakes, to a bona fide gardener, with the ability to learn from successes and failures. She taught me what matters most and imparted the courage to start with minimal yet enough knowledge. When I signed up for her class, I had no inkling of the depth of her wisdom or the impact she would have on my ability to grow vegetables, fruit, herbs, flowers, grass, and even ground cover.

Identifying the fundamentals upon which to build my knowledge moved me from floundering to progressing along the learning curve.

Later, I realized that sound money management, like gardening, could be distilled into three essentials. For successful gardening, the gardener needs good soil, sunlight, and water. In personal finance, if you want to grow wealth, you need to 1) spend less than you earn, 2) make money in ways that do not require daily work, and 3) protect yourself from devastating loss. In short: save, invest, and protect.

The Learning Curve Takeaway

Learning new concepts and applying them in the real world is challenging. Discover the approach that works best for you. Focus on the fundamentals and build your acumen on this foundation.

The First Essential: Do This One Thing

7

Lay the Foundation

THE NOTION OF GARDENING essentials inspired a structure for sharing my understanding of personal finance.

My instructor's emphasis on good soil reminded me of the principle of spending less than I earned. If I failed at this part, nothing else mattered.

As a beginner, I had learned where to focus: Identify good soil and start there. Further, stay away from researching innovative methods, buying fancy tools, or finding the perfect approach to gardening.

Likewise, if you're a beginner in managing finances, start with the simple act of spending less than you earn. Stay away from elaborate investing systems, complex trading methods, savings programs that require buying insurance, debt payoff schemes that involve borrowing money, and sophisticated tools that mysteriously manage your money.

After the gardening lesson and emphasis on what matters most, I returned home and pinpointed a plot in my yard for a garden. It already had great soil, a place where a composting of leaves and grass had happened through lawn neglect. In addition, this spot received sun all day, the ingredient necessary for growing tomatoes, a feat recognized in my region as the epitome of gardening prowess.

Could gardening and growing wealth be simple, distilled to three essentials? Or are these essentials—dirt, sun, and water for gardening and save, invest, and protect for growing wealth—merely the necessities to start the journey on a long learning curve?

8

Act Natural

I AM NOT A natural at gardening. There's no way I could learn without instruction.

I am, however, a saver by nature. My tendency was inborn and nurtured by my parents, who were children during the Great Depression.

My first memory of saving was as a five-year-old, playing with kids in my neighborhood.

My friends included a freckle-faced girl I will call Kate, who decided to dispense small pieces of chocolate candy one day. She counted them aloud to the kids standing in a circle awaiting her gift.

I did not want to eat the candy immediately, so I pocketed a few for later.

To be fair in her distribution, Kate paused and asked how many pieces of candy everyone had eaten. During this investigation, she discovered my stash of chocolate. She refused to give me more until I ate what I had received.

I cannot remember whether I caved and consumed the candy or stood my ground and saved whatever I had in my pocket for later. But I do recall this: I liked to save. Other people did not love to save as I did.

For much of my life, I divided people into two categories: savers and spenders. I believed spenders could never get ahead financially because, well, they always spent more than they earned.

Here's what I learned: I was wrong.

More specifically, I came to realize that some, perhaps many, spenders focus on earning more, not spending less. Those who cultivate their earning capabilities build wealth when they recognize spending weaknesses and find ways to set aside money from their paychecks and business profits.

Throughout my childhood and beyond, I persisted as a saver, though I did not have a specific goal inspiring my thrift. I opened a savings account when I attended elementary school. I rode my bike to a branch bank to deposit money earned through summer jobs in junior high and high school. I set aside college earnings for whatever might surface as a need or opportunity, such as a road trip across the United States, a summer in

London with my sister when she lived overseas, or the down payment on my first car, needed for my first real job.

I set aside money because saving brought me joy. It gave me a sense of accomplishment and control over my future. It also benefited my financial journey.

Further, encouragement to save for a rainy day was a perennial message in my growing-up years—my mom often spoke about it. As a child who thought very literally, I figured having a few extra dollars would allow me to go to the movies when it rained, an alternative to playing outside. (I had not yet begun to consider the value of rain in nourishing a garden and sustaining life.)

Later, I understood rainy days in terms of job losses, economic recessions, hiring freezes, slowing business, and stock market declines. These events were not abstract ideas or circumstances happening to other people. They manifested themselves as high unemployment after college graduation, workplace layoffs, and the drying up of client calls during recessions.

Whether I treated them as literal or figurative, rainy days were inevitable. Spending less than I earned in anticipation of these happenings—and saving for them—proved beneficial to my well-being.

9

Adjust

GROWING MONEY IN A bank account as a child and teenager delighted me. But saving while subsidized by my parents and saving while supporting myself materialized as two different challenges.

A few months after college graduation, I landed a job as a financial analyst for a regional bank headquartered in a small North Carolina town. The company extended free checking services to its employees, but this arrangement had a catch. My employer enforced a policy about checks returned for nonsufficient funds (NSFs). The first incident would result in disciplinary action; three bounced checks meant I would be fired. Reconciling bank account statements with my check register, a paper trail of activity, became a necessary habit.

To spend less than I earned and avoid NSFs, I lived simply. My apartment was situated far from what I knew as civilization. Evening entertainment involved getting together with friends or watching the one broadcast channel available at my apartment, which did not offer cable television or yet-to-be-invented streaming services.

Dealing with basic living expenses was relatively easy. My cost of living was low. My paycheck covered my portion of rent and utility bills for an apartment I shared with a roommate, car payments, insurance, groceries, and lunches with coworkers.

But before my paychecks hit my bank account, the margin was often slim, one dollar or less. I strove to maintain this edge and my standing with my employer.

The upside to my apartment in the middle of nowhere was its location, about a half hour's drive to the Blue Ridge Parkway, part of the National Park Service.

My main leisure activity became hiking with friends. A hike on trails along the parkway, in a nearby state park, or on a friend's land would be the highlight of my week. Occasionally, we would splurge to pay for canoeing in the summer or skiing in the winter. We were all broke, mostly, or eager to save, and we tended to spend merely what the least wealthy of us could afford.

My friends were the secret to my eventual firm financial footing. In addition to helping me spend less, they united for a group revelation about the dangers of credit cards.

I kept fixed expenses low and paid bills on time, but I also used credit cards. I charged purchases of work-related clothing and kitchen items for meal preparation. These purchases helped me earn a living and control expenses.

I felt justified in using the cards because the things I bought consisted primarily of items I needed. Also, I never missed a payment.

Even though card acceptance wasn't widespread (grocery stores hadn't yet started accepting cards for payments), and my card limit was relatively low, a couple of thousand dollars, the accumulated debt presented a problem.

One particular credit card statement shook me up. I had noticed the timeline for paying off the card if I made minimum payments only. Though the document listed the time in months, there were *so many* months: The payoff would take *years*.

My friends and I came to a critical realization about credit card debt. We were in our twenties, college graduates, and working in professional positions. While the cost of living remained low in our small town, our salaries reflected this reality. None of us lived luxuriously, shopped as a form of therapy, joined country clubs, or took expensive vacations. For the first few years of our post-college life, we used our paychecks to cover basic living costs, plus things like retirement plan contributions. At the same time, we financed our start-up costs for the real world with car loans and credit cards for other significant expenses.

Several of us had gathered in a friend's apartment, when the topic of finances and the future came up. After a couple of years of working and living on our own, we were starting to consider life beyond survival mode. Someone introduced the topic of credit card debt and the amount of time it would take to pay off balances if we continued with minimum payments.

Discovering that we all were facing similar financial battles emboldened us to swim against the tide. Most of us worked for the bank, so we grasped the financial implications of unending credit card debt. It would keep us treading water, so to speak, financially, and prevent us from reaching the shore and taking steps toward saving for our future. We realized controlling our monthly expenses with credit cards would not end well. In fact, the problem would never end if we did not stop using credit cards. So, we stopped—I did, anyway—right then.

As a gardener, you may have experienced early success. Your first efforts may have coincided with a season that enjoyed no early or late frosts, the right amount of rain and sunshine, and dirt filled with healthy elements for supporting growth. Later, maybe a late frost damaged your crop, the soil needed more nutrients to allow vegetables to thrive, or your area experienced a drought. You may not have been prepared the first time you encountered these problems, but eventually, you learned how to adjust and minimize their impact on your garden's production.

You may have had a similar learning experience in the financial realm, wherein you recognized shortcomings in the past, resolved change for the future, and implemented a system to deal with overspending (or underearning). If you've never overspent, and you saved easily at all stages of life, bravo. If not, however, know that even natural savers, good with money, find adapting to new circumstances challenging.

While I made up my mind to stop using my credit card, I also had to deal with credit balances from a department store, a dress shop, and even my dentist, who had allowed me to pay for several sessions of dental work over time. I was stirred to avoid all spending, even on purchases with the potential to benefit my finances in the long run.

With this resolve to eliminate debt, I devised a plan. It involved paying off balances, freeing money previously allocated to monthly payments, and applying the excess to savings.

10

Celebrate

MY PLAN WORKED. I eliminated my credit habit, cut my spending, and began to save.

My crowning achievement was setting up a direct deposit from my paycheck to a savings account. I diverted twenty dollars per month away from immediate needs to long-term ones. Not only had I embraced saving as a financial essential, but I also figured out how to save as an adult.

This move represented a milestone. It reinforced my desire to progress in my financial acumen. Success deserves to be celebrated, whether the endeavor involves finance or gardening—even when the results are meager, a spindly carrot or a sole zucchini.

When I told a coworker about saving twenty dollars per month, she suggested twenty-five dollars per paycheck as a better choice. She reasoned that my account balance could accrue in increments of one hundred dollars at a quicker pace.

This person often complained about the lack of money in her household, so I didn't want to take instruction from someone who struggled.

Also, I knew my financial situation more intimately than she did and believed that I may not have been able to afford the amount she recommended.

I ignored her advice and continued to applaud my achievement.

I felt awkward when an acquaintance familiar with my gardening efforts asked me about my flowers. I had spoken of vegetables only, but she seemed to be envisioning my yard bursting with color like hers. *Flowers, uh, no, I haven't yet grown those, unless you count the wildflower seeds that I spread near the edge of our lawn in a muddy, often leaf-covered area to prevent erosion.*

Likewise, you may have been proud of paying off a car loan or opening a 401(k) account, and then a neighbor, coworker, or in-law tells you about his mortgage payoff years ago or the brokerage account she started in college. You may have been thrilled at saving 5 percent of your income, capturing a 3 percent employer match on your 401(k), or growing your portfolio by 7 percent in the last year. Then a friend suggests 10 percent as the right amount to save and claims to have earned 20 percent in annual investment returns.

Your response to these brags and suggestions can be like mine: ignore them and celebrate anyway.

I had unlocked the key to financial freedom. Spend one cent less than I earned. Spending less allowed me to save for the inevitable rainy day.

This practice started the compounding of interest in my favor. After learning to set aside a penny, I saved a dime, then more as my income increased, and I paid off my debt. Clearing the first obstacle had posed a challenge, but done once, the next became easier to overcome.

This solitary skill, spending less than earned, practiced over and over, reset, again and again, formed the foundation of my financial freedom. After experiencing adulthood for more than a few minutes, though, I would encounter more hurdles—some predictable, some random.

11

Plan, Then Manage

Spend less than I earn is a simple concept that can feel complex to execute. The reason is straightforward: Paychecks arrive at different intervals than payment due dates.

For example, when single and renting an apartment, I managed my budget without a high salary due to my simple circumstances. Bills like rent, car payments, and utility expenses came monthly, for one person.

After I married and had children, planning became more complicated. Expenses now included annual life insurance bills, income taxes on investments, car repairs, medical bills not covered by insurance, home repairs, school photos, book fairs, birthday parties, and Christmas presents for an extended family. The process of spending less became a moving target, requiring sustained and creative effort.

My work in finance and accounting helped. I learned to think in terms of yearly expenses and to say words like "annualize." My colleagues and I prepared annual budgets by noting monthly bills, yearly charges, and one-off expenses. We totaled these and determined annual amounts for various categories, which we called line items. Then, we created monthly budgets by dividing by twelve. (Occasionally, someone would slot an August-only expense in August, which is just as reasonable as spreading out the cost over the entire year. However, this move was viewed as risky as the invoice may not arrive and become due for payment in the expected month.)

This stint in accounting taught me a couple of things about budgeting, whether at home or at work. First, there is a comprehensive process where you lay out all the expenses and eliminate the ones you cannot afford based on either your income or your boss's constraints. The second is budgeting implementation, in which you assure cash is available to pay bills as they come due. Both practices are necessary. However, they are distinct functions: budget projections and cash flow management, planning and doing.

A critical component of success is not deviating from your plan. This technique requires not spending if the original budget did not include funding for the desired expenditure and no money is available after reviewing the bank balance and accounting for all the bills in the pipeline.

I applied this accounting approach to my finances by considering all expenses, whether monthly, weekly, or yearly, calculating annual costs, and planning based on the totals. I paid monthly bills from a regular paycheck and set aside money for non-monthly bills. These funds accumulated in a checking account or were transferred to a savings account. When non-monthly bills arrived, I paid them from stored-up funds.

Occasionally, I used tools offered by service providers to convert bills to monthly installments. For example, my utility company offered an equalized payment plan to smooth statement fluctuations based on varying energy usage throughout the year. Likewise, the insurance company allowed me to pay in monthly installments rather than annually. These arrangements often incurred fees, but the ease of paying bills monthly was sometimes worth the small cost.

Thinking back to what matters most in gardening—good soil—I imagine a change in locations would bring similar challenges to budgeting. If I moved every year, I could experiment with my garden plot, but the results wouldn't be helpful as I'd need to start over in a new place the following year. An alternative would require advanced skills: I could learn to test the soil for pH levels and nutrients each year, then amend the soil to cultivate the types of plants I was intending to grow.

I've yet to analyze my soil, even though I've been growing a garden for several years. I started with a good patch of earth, which worked well initially. Later, I added organic soil after a disappointing gardening season. Planting in the same area, year after year, has made it easier to plan and manage my garden.

Consistency brings simplicity, whether in soil for gardening or spending less than earned for growing wealth. I'm not urging you to stay in one house, keep one job, and maintain expenses at one level for the rest of your life. I'm claiming that changing circumstances bring challenges.

If you haven't worked in accounting and detailed planning sounds intimidating, you're not alone. The constant monitoring of expenses can be stressful and mentally taxing, especially when the calculations for spending less than you earn involve a moving target.

Eventually, I came to envision a method of expense control that didn't require the yearly planning that my job in accounting did.

12

Divide, Then Conquer

An acquaintance not as endeared to numbers and still figuring out how to build financial solvency asked me how to control spending when there is so much to spend it on! She mentioned social outings as a special concern. Underlying the question, I believed, was her worry that she might need to become a recluse to balance her budget.

After a few exchanges, I realized the desire to fit in socially and professionally was not my acquaintance's primary concern. Instead, she craved a framework for financial decision-making. What resonated with her was my approach to categorizing expenses as fixed, variable, or discretionary. As long as you earn a living wage, adopting this way of thinking about money removes the burden of day-to-day expense analysis.

Fixed expenses are incurred regularly, often monthly, and persist unless I make significant changes to my life. Rent for an apartment, a thirty-year mortgage, car payments, and certain types of insurance fall into the fixed-expense category.

Variable expenses are for essentials not included in the fixed items. Monthly utility bills and groceries fall under this category. To a certain extent, I can control them. However, though they can be trimmed, they can't be eliminated. For example, to reduce variable expenses, I could turn down the thermostat in the winter or skip snacks at the grocery store.

Discretionary expenses are what I consider expenses for fun. These cover things or experiences like bicycles or kayaking trips. I allow myself to buy them only after paying for essentials, such as food and shelter.

I *could* say that expenses for things like gym memberships and streaming services like Netflix are fixed. The merchants set the prices, which represent steady, recurring charges. Neither are critical to sustaining life or work, however, so I classify them as discretionary expenses, easy to eliminate during a money crisis.

After determining the baseline for sustaining my family and myself (take-home pay less fixed and variable-yet-essential costs), I identify the dollar amount available for discretionary spending and then focus on controlling those expenses. This method of dividing costs into categories makes it easier to conquer the challenge of spending less than earned. In addition, I can expend my brainpower on managing leisure expenses rather than scrutinizing and revisiting all costs regularly.

Fixed, variable, and discretionary concepts relate to sun, soil, and water. All play an essential role in sparking and sustaining growth. The amount of sun available to vegetable gardens and fruit orchards is fixed, depending on their locations, similar to how budgeted dollars allotted for a home mortgage or car payment remain constant. You may adjust these, with significant effort, by cutting down trees and removing structures that block the sun or moving to a new place and selling a car to reduce costs. Generally, gardeners choose where to plant based on the availability of sun, then adjust soil and water.

Soil reminds me of variable expenses. These costs can be tweaked, just as the soil can be amended, a fancy word that means nutrients can be added to improve it or make it better for the types of food you want to grow. For example, I may add compost in varying amounts each year to create a richer environment, which may yield more plentiful vegetables.

Watering suggests a discretionary activity that makes life fuller and more manageable. Generally, I rely on rain to nourish my garden. (I now appreciate those "rainy days," literal ones, anyway.) I may supplement with water from my garden hose to ensure my plants receive enough of this essential, especially during dry periods. Too much rain and water, like excessive discretionary expenses, can pose a problem for certain plants and budgets.

One of the easiest ways to manage money is to be careful about fixed expenses—rent, mortgage, insurance, etc. These are difficult to adjust when life changes, and life continually changes. Focusing on keeping fixed costs low helps assure money is available for fun things, like weekend getaways, and long-term goals, such as a comfortable retirement.

This approach also allows for flexibility. For example, if you want to switch from a high-paying job that requires extensive travel to one with an average salary that gives you weekends at home, you can make this change and still pay your mortgage on time.

On the other hand, many people favor buying a luxurious house and minimizing variable expenses and discretionary spending. Others may focus on earning more to spend, save, invest, and even give more.

There is no single right way to manage or classify all expenses. Further, just because you have a handle on one category does not mean you won't overspend on another without planning. This fixed-variable-discretionary framework, however, brings clarity and ease to the budgeting process.

Find what works for you, whether that is the kind of meticulous planning an accountant might do, a framework emphasizing control of fixed expenses, or something else. Stick with your approach, adjusting and refining it as circumstances change.

Whether growing wealth or growing vegetables, considering the elements together yet managing them separately can yield good results.

13

Control, or Be Controlled

JUST AS SAVING CAME naturally to me, controlling fixed expenses also seemed intuitive and more straightforward than other methods. For example, I controlled these costs by choosing an affordable home.

A friend who grew up on a potato farm told me her dad spoke to her often about quality dirt. My obsession with an affordable home may have been like his emphasis on soil, a foundational element of success.

When my husband and I were young, we bought a beautiful ranch house. The price tag exceeded our anticipated cost, but the mortgage payments remained within our financial reach.

Being a homeowner with house amenities thrilled me. Visits to the laundromat were a thing of the past. I now carried laundry down our hallway to our own washer and dryer. Planning a casual workout was no longer a significant undertaking, as I simply stepped outside and took leisurely walks.

Then I had this weird dream. In it, I was crawling between metal coils, a set above and below me. There seemed to be no way out except through endless pathways. I felt trapped.

After several instances of the dream, I recognized the space where I was crawling as my home's attic. The sense of being stuck lessened as I realized that movement was possible in my dream, though limited. I could travel within the confines of the narrow space between the coils in the attic, but I remained away from the house's pleasures, the spacious deck and cozy den. My ability to inch along reassured me that, eventually, I would complete and exit this maze.

My husband and I had bought the house because I had grown tired of our rental. Problems abounded when we rented. Our former landlord said he would take care of the rental home's yard maintenance if he could increase our rent. We gladly agreed to pay more, but he failed to deliver on the maintenance; instead, the grass grew tall and fall leaves piled up.

A promised refrigerator appeared, but in a miniature version, swallowed by the space allotted to this appliance. The lock to the outside storage room housing the dryer never worked properly, making laundry a challenging chore in the winter and the area insecure year-round.

When appliances broke down, the landlord dillydallied in making repairs, though we delivered our rent checks on time. Worse, he would not allow us to make improvements even if we paid for them.

The most straightforward path out of the landlord dilemma was to buy our own house and deal with any problems ourselves. We looked at dozens of homes in a price range we had agreed upon. One place seemed to have serious foundation problems. Many others needed costly repairs.

Eventually, we decided to consider houses in a higher price range. The price of what would become our home exceeded what we had intended to pay when we started the process. However, there were no apparent repairs needed. The owners had remodeled the kitchen and equipped it with new, full-size appliances. It contained three bedrooms, two baths, a deck, a screened-in porch, and a two-car garage. The property was near schools, work, and the local community college.

We could afford the home because housing prices were reasonable, depressed even. We lived in a small town that had suffered economic downturns, such as company shutdowns, consolidations, and bankruptcies.

Through our efforts and a real estate agent's help, a purchase offer was extended and accepted, a mortgage loan located, the contract signed, and the deal done.

Even though we bought a more expensive house than anticipated, we borrowed less than the banks were willing to lend to us. Making the monthly payment was not demanding in terms of our paychecks covering the bill. It totaled the same amount as our former rent plus our two car payments, debt we had recently settled.

Still, taking on a mortgage represented a big financial step. Perhaps my psyche was unprepared for this weightiness, as the recurring dream about being trapped started shortly after we bought the house.

At first, I did not link the mortgage with the feeling of being trapped inside my home. Only after I consulted a dream dictionary did I make the connection. Then, after realizing my subconscious was agonizing over this long-term agreement, the dream stopped.

I was grateful we had not overextended ourselves, or my nightmare may have become real. With this message received from my subconscious, my desire to keep fixed costs low became even more ingrained.

14

Eliminate Fixed Expenses

My husband and I intended on staying longer in the ranch house, but a work-related relocation prompted us to sell it. We sold our first home—two days after putting it on the market! Less than two years after taking on our first mortgage, we paid off the loan.

It was in the yard of that home where I first tried to create a different outdoor space. I planted wildflower seeds I hoped would create a colorful ground cover in a shaded, uneven, often muddy area of the backyard. We lived there long enough to know that my growing attempt failed, but not long enough to try anything else.

We bought and sold another home before settling in a house with the yard where I planted my current garden. Here, we paid off the mortgage in about fifteen years.

Early mortgage payoff, or payoff at all, is controversial in certain personal finance circles. A few deem it wise to avoid debt altogether. Many strive to eliminate debt as soon as possible. Others believe it is foolish to pay off a mortgage early or at all when interest rates are low, because you could generate higher returns through investing.

I love doing the math to help me make money decisions, whether debt payoff or stock selection. When I want to relax, I fire up a spreadsheet.

There are many elements to the mortgage payoff vs investing equation. These include the borrowing rate, generally a fixed interest rate, and investment returns, which can be anticipated but not guaranteed. The tax benefits of itemizing mortgage interest (favoring a mortgage) and reducing income through retirement account contributions (favoring investing) can also be considered.

Further, other financial priorities, such as high-interest debt payoff, insurance purchases, and even discretionary spending, compete with putting money toward a quicker payoff of your mortgage principal or building your investment portfolio.

Additional considerations include the certainty of income and income levels. For example, a commissioned sales representative, whose income varies from month to month, may strategize differently from an essential government employee with a stable monthly paycheck.

What tilted my decision toward choosing the accelerated fifteen-year mortgage: The interest rate on my loan was more than I could earn in a savings account. Sure, I could possibly make more through investing. But my husband and I were heavily invested in stocks, and I did not see the need to take on more risk. (My comparison investments were *not* the S&P 500, the top five hundred companies in the US combined, or individual stocks. Instead, they were fixed-income assets like FDIC-insured bank accounts, which paid interest lower than my mortgage rate.)

By opting for a fifteen-year mortgage, with its higher monthly payment than a thirty-year version, I increased our family's fixed expenses. This move reduced the amount available for discretionary spending in our thirties and forties; we planned to enjoy lower fixed costs in our fifties and beyond. It seemed an easy way to automate finances, similar to diverting funds from a monthly paycheck to a savings account, brokerage account, or employer-sponsored retirement account.

For those considering a shorter-term mortgage or accelerated payment schedule, there is a drawback to this approach. Your money will be tied up in an illiquid asset, your house, which generates cash only when sold, unless you take out a home equity line or second mortgage, defeating the purpose of paying down the mortgage quickly. That is, early payments on a mortgage do not yield cash flow benefits until the loan is paid off completely.

Eventually, being debt free conveyed a sense of freedom. However, I did not experience this when I made the last mortgage payment. That feeling would come later.

I would feel that freedom whenever there was a global economic blip, a major worldwide crisis, layoffs at work (something my husband and I experienced six times during our careers), and whenever I sensed a need to alter an aspect of my life without going broke. During those periods, a paid-in-full house comforted me.

Today, home-related bills, such as property taxes and insurance, persist. But in times of financial or personal distress, I feel grateful to live in a home I own free and clear.

As a side note about math and spreadsheets, I run the numbers to inform my decisions, not to dictate them. Likewise, you may grow certain vegetables because you love them, not merely because a harvest helps you avoid high costs at the grocery store.

15

Designate, When Possible

ANOTHER ADVANTAGE OF LOW fixed expenses (made possible through an affordable home) is a likely surplus of money for saving and investing. Again, this approach means you can take advantage of compounding growth.

When I began saving, I didn't have a grand vision with well-defined, long-term economic goals for my entire life, about which financial advisors would query me. I believed more was better than less and that when opportunities arose or crises appeared, money would help.

I figured I would need to save for the big items people talk about, such as retirement, college for the kids, and health care. These happened to be categories for which the IRS (Internal Revenue Service) allows tax breaks through "qualified" accounts. I could save on income taxes by using special savings and investment accounts for retirement, college, health care, and later, charitable giving.

Just as you may designate one area of your land for blueberry bushes, another for vegetables, and yet another for flowers, you can select where to allocate your money. If you know ahead of time where your flowers will be planted and where your dollars for retirement will be stored, the sowing and growing process can be less stressful than trying to figure things out at the start of each season, again and again.

Since my start in investing, I've learned a few things about saving for the future. One of them is that many people are like me in that they don't have a firm grasp on life goals at age twenty-five or even thirty-five, so queries about specific plans are often ineffective.

As an alternative, conversations centered on your values, fears, and aspirations about life and money can be productive. They can help you figure out where to put money and understand what money can and cannot buy. Still, the more you know about money-related goals and the more you can save within designated accounts for specific purposes, the better.

Spending for college, health care, and even giving is simpler when the money comes from designated accounts. Emotionally, it's easier to let go of money that I've decided ahead of time to spend for a definite goal. The final step is simply handling the paperwork, albeit digitally.

Eventually, with robust savings and investments, I was able to pay ongoing bills from regular paychecks and designated accounts. For example, I could pay college tuition using money from qualified college savings plans and health care bills from a health savings account (HSA).

Planning for income, expenses, and cash flow became even more crucial when I began using long-term savings in addition to drawing on paychecks and business earnings. I needed to align sources with designated purposes and make sure cash was available at the right time.

For example, not only did I anticipate college expenses, but I later needed to ensure that funds were transferred from the college investment account to my checking account when the bills came due. The root of this entire process was initiating a direct deposit of twenty dollars from my paycheck to my savings account years ago.

16

Steward Resources

Just as saving and spending intentionally may beneficially impact your finances, there can be a deeper purpose to spending less than you earn. This practice frees money to invest, creates a margin in a budget for generosity, and encourages broader stewardship.

This idea of preserving resources started with my husband and I, newly married, laughing about tinsel. Our parents had saved strands year after year. As kids, we were both charged with extracting tinsel from Christmas trees and storing it for future use.

Our parents did not know each other during their childhood years. But all four of them were children during the Great Depression and seemed to live with similar money mindsets, which could be distilled into "Waste not, want not."

My husband and I, however, reasoned we could buy new tinsel every year. The time saved by abandoning our parents' practice would be worth more than the money saved by its removal, storage, and retrieval each Christmas season.

What lessons did tinsel saving impart? Did the pennies saved, or perhaps dollars, make a difference? Or was it a habit to keep what you have and never toss anything away? At first, it seemed like a remnant of the past.

Years later, I recognized another meaning from our parents' money lessons.

In a small closet tucked under a set of stairs in my house, I hold items from Christmases past in preparation for Christmases future. Messy substances like tinsel and glitter are not included. However, there is tissue paper, carefully placed and sealed in plastic bags, so pesky silverfish do not join our celebrations. There are also gift bags of all sizes stuffed in a box, so many that I may never shop for bags again.

Having bags and tissue paper handy keeps me from driving to the store, wandering around, choosing the perfect bag and matching paper, picking up more items, hauling everything home, and tossing out what remains or storing for later. The lesson from my parents became clear: Saving stuff is not only about money. It is also about preserving resources.

Growing and consuming produce from my garden uses fewer transportation resources than traditional grocery shopping, in which I buy cherries from Washington and grapes from Chile. It may help reduce emissions associated with airfreight, ocean containers, and tractor trailers. Expanding my growing capacity with a small fruit orchard in my backyard has attracted birds and pollinators, supporting food diversity—not only for me but for others.

The First Essential Takeaway

UNDERSTAND AND MASTER THE one thing that matters most in achieving your goals, whether evaluating dirt or controlling expenses. Never underestimate the power of simple actions. Be kind to yourself as you learn and adapt to changing circumstances.

The Second Essential: Reap More Than You Sow

17

Begin

After dealing with this first essential—spending less than I earned—I moved to the next, making money that isn't generated by daily labor. To achieve financial freedom, I knew I had to create or acquire assets to generate the income or produce the goods and services I needed to live.

Assets may include a portfolio of stocks and bonds, a vegetable garden or fruit orchard, an annuity, a creative expression such as a song or book, a patented invention, or real estate. Potential payoffs include capital gains, ripe produce, interest, royalties, and monthly rental income. Generating yield takes a combination of time, effort, and money.

Compared to a traditional job or consulting gig, here's what's different and important about these sources of prosperity: The outcomes are not aligned with effort the way a paycheck matches a workweek.

Cultivating sources of income independent of an employer or business and growing a garden require effort but not necessarily daily activity.

For example, a blueberry bush in my backyard yielded fruit without my day-to-day involvement last summer. Besides arranging for the purchase and planting of the bush years ago, I snapped and removed a few twigs earlier in the year, a process known as pruning. With this minimal time investment, I received a daily harvest for weeks.

Likewise, I can harvest income without daily work. I may expend effort, but after the initial investment, I hope to reap more than I sow.

Soon after settling into our ranch house, the one void of wildflower ground cover, I began acquiring shares of my utility company through a direct-investment program offered to its customers.

At the time, buying stocks through a broker was expensive, often costing hundreds of dollars for a single transaction. When I noticed the insert in my utility bill touting this program, I signed up. There were no fees for buying shares and a small fee to sell them. My investing habit began.

I opened an investment account with the minimum requirement. I can't recall the dollar amount today, but it was relatively low, perhaps one hundred dollars. After the account was set up, I periodically mailed in checks to buy more shares. The investment program administrator pooled my money with other investors, purchased shares on my behalf, and then assigned those shares to my account.

Emboldened by the ease of buying shares in a specific company, I decided to expand my investing horizons. I bought shares of mutual funds directly from the fund companies Fidelity (now Fidelity Investments) and Janus (now Janus Henderson). I opened accounts with the minimum required amounts and then purchased more shares whenever I had extra money.

Through these arrangements, I avoided the transaction fees typical of traditional brokerage firms at the time. Just as significant, I enjoyed randomly investing small amounts; the actual number would depend on my bank balance and the minimums for initial and subsequent investments.

I paid little attention to share prices or company values. My attention was focused on accumulating shares and growing wealth, with no aim other than to begin.

When I would buy shares at the market price each month, I may have paid too much, snagged them at a bargain, or purchased them at precisely the right price compared to the business's worth. When I acquired shares over a long period, say several years, my costs per share became averages of the price fluctuations.

Eventually, I learned the financial lingo for this process: dollar-cost averaging or systematic investing. The irregular intervals of my purchases may have disqualified my approach from being considered "systematic," but the methodology of buying over time was similar.

(Note that financial professional purists may consider dollar-cost averaging a stock acquisition strategy that exists only in juxtaposition with lump-sum investing. But I believe the practice is just as applicable to the beginning investor with modest amounts available monthly to spend on stocks as it is to an investor who can't decide whether to buy shares all at once or spread purchases to control risk and avoid buying just before a market downturn.)

A few years after my start, I became disillusioned with the utility company because of its leadership. A person of power and influence recommended shareholder actions, intimating that there would be widespread benefit, which were revealed later to enrich a handful of owners only, me not included. I still believed in investing but began to consider more than the relative ease of purchasing shares.

18

Do What Works for You

To grow wealth, I focused on investing in stocks and funds that held stocks. As a business major who enjoyed analyzing financial statements and evaluating companies, I believed this path was a natural choice.

My experiences with the financially free also shaped my mindset. As a young adult, I had known one independently wealthy person, a woman who had made her fortune investing in a chain of grocery stores started by a local businessperson in a small city in North Carolina. I noticed she stood her ground on matters important to her, even when her stance was unpopular and risky. Investing offered a pathway to financial security *and* personal freedom. I aimed to develop my skills in these areas.

Investing in the stock market seemed like the preferred route to financial stability for everyday people, particularly those uninterested in running a business, starting a side hustle, or buying real estate. Compared to other wealth-building methods, investing appeared simpler and less time-consuming. I could set up brokerage accounts and buy stocks, contribute to employer-sponsored retirement plans and choose mutual funds, and then watch for signs of growth.

However, there are many more ways to grow wealth and generate income without working every day.

Several years ago, a friend told me his mom was worried because he was not investing and saving for retirement. He was single and had no children or dependents.

I contemplated his situation and asked about his pension plan—upon retirement he would receive pension payments because he worked for a federal agency.

I explained that the aim of retirement investing was to accumulate wealth, which he could later draw upon to create a stream of income. His pension produced the same thing as investments: cash to pay bills for essential expenses and cover the cost of discretionary extras. The pension plan would allow him to skip steps (saving, investing, accumulating wealth through investment growth, selling investments, transferring cash from his retirement accounts to his checking account) and go straight to receiving income in retirement.

A pension-like herb grows in my garden. I planted parsley seeds a few years ago. Since then, it has multiplied itself, persisted through frosts and summer heat, and continues to produce leaves. Periodically, I harvest these leafy greens and add them to my breakfast smoothies. The taste is nonexistent, so they do not add excitement to my day, but they serve the purpose of providing nutrients.

I could spend money and exert energy each season cultivating tastier and more diverse greens, just as my friend could add more exciting investments to his retirement portfolio. Skipping these steps is fine, as our needs are met with parsley and pensions without extra effort or risk.

Before our conversation, my friend most likely understood how a pension worked and the point of investing. His mom's concern had compelled him to reflect on his situation and consider whether he should begin investing.

Investing makes sense in many scenarios. However, my friend was not risking poverty in retirement by not opening an investment account, especially if he did not accumulate debt.

The most significant disadvantage to his pension was the lack of access to large sums of cash; he could not buy a new car or renovate a kitchen spontaneously. Instead, he would need to save or borrow for big purchases. The clear advantage of his pension was a steady flow of income for life, guaranteed by the US government.

Another downside to his pension is that something could happen to the federal government, affecting its ability to generate paychecks for its former employees. However, if that happened, he would have more to worry about than a pension.

Developing more than one way to generate cash without daily work makes sense, whether through rental income on real estate, dividends on stock investments, or royalties from a book series. If my friend had the motivation and extra money to invest, I would have encouraged him to do so.

You may enjoy annuals, for which you prepare the soil, sow seeds, and reap for a season. Likewise, you may revel in your daily work for a nonprofit, government entity, or business (either your own or someone else's), exercising your talents and making the world a better place through your efforts—while also earning income. But, at some point, it's wise to cultivate things that will grow and produce for many years without much ongoing effort.

19

Discard Misconceptions

After talking to my friend about his pension, I realized it is easy to develop misconceptions about financial freedom and the best way to achieve it. These ideas may come from direct experiences, beliefs passed down by family members, or stories told about the rich.

Likewise, certain kinds of gardens may evoke stereotypes of the sort of person who cultivates them.

The owner of a formal garden suggests a person of means who employs others to manage shrubbery shaping and flower blooming. A person with an elegant garden may be concerned with entertaining guests and looking beautiful, not with the day-to-day activities of scrutinizing bills and providing for a family.

A vegetable gardener may conjure the image of a diligent worker. This person may be frugal, someone who plants in hopes of saving money on grocery bills.

Just as stereotypical are the images of those who live financially secure and free lives. It's a myth that business ownership is the fastest, most reliable path to independent wealth. The opposing myth claims that working for someone else means always being broke.

There are seeds of truth in the idea that the wealthiest are business owners and the poorest are lifelong employees. An owner may structure a business to generate a high income and create an asset to fund life and dreams after retiring or selling the company. An employee may never be paid according to their true worth and fear leaving one job for a better one because of personal obligations, debt loads, or both.

Being an employee, however, does not prevent someone from doing well financially. Those fortunate enough to receive a steady paycheck, access to health insurance, a retirement plan match, and paid days off may fare better than a business owner who struggles to make payroll, collect receivables, and offer excellent employee benefits.

Savings from paychecks can build a portfolio of stocks or provide seed money to purchase rental properties. Leisure time not spent taking care of endless business tasks may provide the freedom to create intellectual property generating royalties for years to come, long after saying goodbye to an employer.

Misconceptions may prevent you from capitalizing on your strengths and growing wealth. You may start a business, thinking it's essential to fortifying your financial position when you prefer a steady job and already earn a good income. Or you may stick with an unsatisfying job, believing that you can't find similar insurance benefits on your own. I'm not trying to advise you on the best and surefire ways to become financially independent. Rather, I'm urging to find your own path to financial success, drawing on your unique capabilities, desires, and circumstances.

20

Refine Your Style

As for my husband and me, accumulating wealth happened more smoothly as employees of companies with retirement plans, stock programs, and generous health benefits. Later, my experience working independently gave me the tools to sharpen my investing skills.

As my account balances grew and discount brokers emerged, I began buying shares in lump sums rather than investing a specific amount monthly.

This approach was riskier, or felt that way, because I bought shares at the going price rather than spreading out my purchases and smoothing my costs. Financial research has declared lump-sum investing as the winner over dollar-cost averaging. That is, investing a bunch of money at one point in time is more likely to give you higher investment returns than buying shares over time. But research looks at overall statistics, not individual results, and ignores the emotional distress of loss. Eventually, I learned to reconcile the two, financial truths and fear.

When I started buying stocks using the lump-sum method, I focused on companies I liked that appeared to be growing. I've read that investing in individual stocks and, worse, merely what you prefer, rarely delivers success. My technique, refined over the years, uses attractiveness as a starting point for my investment decisions, not as the sole data point.

Likewise, as a gardener, you may begin planning a garden based on personal preferences or simply what's available in terms of seeds and starter plants. Next, you may winnow your selections based on your regional growing zone, soil composition, availability of sun, and other factors. So, while you grow what you like, you sow with forethought.

I learned to apply my financial knowledge to evaluating a stock pick, along with characteristics that would influence a company's performance in the long run. My decision framework isn't flawless, but it helps me avoid significant losses.

What do I consider when making an investment decision? Mainly, I focus on buying good companies at reasonable prices. (While this approach seems obvious, it's easy to develop a fear of missing out on exciting businesses with ever-rising share prices. Investors paying sky-high prices for unprofitable businesses led to the burst of the dotcom bubble in the late 1990s.)

Ideally, these companies offer products and services that allow their customers to grow and prosper, whether those are individuals or corporations. As a result, these products and services may be integrated into business operations or consumers' day-to-day lives in a way that positively impacts the world, even if such adoption was not necessarily what company founders and executive teams predicted.

Just as essential are treating employees and vendors fairly, complying with environmental guidelines, and being respected in the communities where they operate. (Asking your friends and neighbors about the working conditions at their employers can be one way of assessing corporate ethics.)

The stories the companies tell the world ought to sync with their financials. For example, when a company asserts that it creates premium products and thrives in its industry, this can be verified by a high gross margin and positive cash flow. (You can find this information by looking at company financial statements—income statements, balance sheets, and cash flow statements—found by entering the company's name or trading symbol in the dashboard of your brokerage firm's website.)

Companies that have weathered storms are attractive. Crises may have included economic recessions, shifts in consumer habits or moods, new legislation, or global events with a lasting impact on demand and operations. Surviving and prospering during these occasions indicates resilience built into the employee culture and management mindset.

Such companies often strive to improve their services and design products to meet ever-changing market demand while staying true to their missions. For example, a business designing and producing artificial intelligence for gaming may later apply this technology to self-driving vehicles. Likewise, a gardener may focus on growing food, starting with vegetables and then expanding to fruits and grains.

I'm drawn to companies that own tangible assets, like production plants, distribution facilities, and equipment. If another company wants to compete with them, it needs forethought and investment, which makes the company with assets more valuable in my eyes. But spending loads of money on infrastructure and improvements can signal a constant drain on cash, so I love to see excess cash available after capital spending in the cash flow statement.

What's also appealing is a company with more than one signature product. Its fortunes do not rise or fall on a single idea that may be popular and innovative one day and forgotten and outdated the next.

Lastly, it's desirable that sales and finance people at the company talk. Signs of healthy communication include enough cash to pay the bills and enough debt to leverage the strength of the business, but not so much to weigh it down in difficult times.

Company executives use excess cash to enhance the business or return it to shareholders in the form of dividends. They invest in their employees, promote a fair workplace, pay average or above-average wages, and offer exceptional benefits. They control expenses, not so stringently as to choke operations, yet not so freely that managers run wild with spending. They maintain healthy profit margins, allowing the company to operate and do good in the world.

Over time, my account balances grew. I matured and realized an impeccable company with flawless leadership was rarer than I had earlier supposed. I started to make investing decisions based less on the details and more on a broader interpretation of the scout rule that told me to leave a place in better condition than I found it.

Instead of asking myself, *Is this business perfect?* I wondered, *Does the company make the world a better place?*

21

Invest for the World You Want

THERE ARE MANY WAYS companies enrich the world, just as there are many ways plants benefit the earth. When I began gardening, I focused on nurturing fruits and vegetables. I shunned what I considered non-functional plants, like flowers. I believed in allocating my time and effort to things that could reap specific, measurable returns, like a basket of tomatoes or a bowl of blueberries. Later, I learned about the value of flowers, not merely for their beauty (which would be enough reason to grow them) but also for their contributions to pollination and biodiversity. Now, I'm not quick to judge the usefulness of a plant until I consider its multiple facets, including benefits of which I'm not yet aware, similar to my evaluation of businesses.

Some businesses create innovative products that reduce strain on the earth's resources. Many offer services that allow people to live better lives through greater access to education, health care, and transportation. Some provide competitive pay and excellent working conditions to an ever-growing team of diverse employees. Investing in businesses that benefit their owners, employees, and communities is worthy but challenging.

A chance meeting at a cycling event in Iowa reinforced this notion. A woman wearing a North Carolina bike jersey said she had worked for what she believed were "merchants of death" when she lived in the state years ago.

I had lined up next to her to buy breakfast at one of the many vendors supplying food, beverages, and supplies for RAGBRAI (the Register's Annual Great Bicycle Ride Across Iowa). The event attracts more than ten thousand cyclists each year. I had traveled from North Carolina, where my fellow cyclist once lived and worked.

Her reference resonated. I wondered, then verified, that she meant a major employer that processed, marketed, and distributed tobacco products.

I sensed twinges of both regret and relief from her. She acknowledged that if she had stayed longer, she could have collected more stock from the company and become rich faster. But instead, she escaped profiting from cancer and death.

The legacy of tobacco covers extremes in my mind: distress and prosperity.

As an investor, I do not wrestle with whether to buy shares of tobacco companies. My family enjoys longevity, and I practice as many healthy habits as possible and abstain from harmful ones like smoking. I was hospitalized as an infant with a respiratory illness, surviving only due to heavy doses of antibiotics. I'll offer an easy *no* to the question about including such a company in my portfolio.

On the other hand, if I evaluated an investment from the perspective of social benefits, such as worker pay, workplace diversity, employee benefits, and positive community impact, I might draw a different conclusion.

Employees in all disciplines of this company seemed to earn high wages, bringing prosperity to many in the city and surrounding towns. In addition, comprehensive health care coverage through a health maintenance organization has been part of the compensation package, possibly increasing workers' expectations for quality health care in this region.

The wealth generated by the company has enriched the community in profound ways. Company executives and their families funded the start of a medical school, now the area's largest employer, with a regional teaching hospital, trauma center, and biomedical research facilities. Foundations started by family members of the founders and key executives now offer grant funds to organizations combatting systemic poverty and racial inequity in housing.

I will not argue whether the good done by the company outweighs the bad. I will assert they sit side by side.

When I contemplate socially responsible investing, ESG (environmental, social, and governance) investing, impact investing, or one of its iterations, I realize a simple checklist does not reveal the distinctions that may cause me to qualify or eliminate a company for consideration. A business may do well in environmental issues yet fail in social ones.

A corporation may excel in employee benefits and community outreach yet produce, market, and distribute a product that addicts and harms its customers.

It may be possible to identify companies sharing my values to include them in my portfolio; however, the process demands more research, soul searching, and due diligence than impact scorecards indicate.

In the past year, I've looked for opportunities to invest in renewable energy. I hope to find a profitable company with an environmentally friendly and sustainable model of generating, storing, and distributing energy. I have envisioned the ideal candidate as a business started in the last five to ten years with promising financial records and innovative technologies.

However, what I've uncovered to date is that this company lives only in my imagination. The profitable businesses with renewable energy sources are often corporations previously focused on fossil fuels. There's a possibility that I'll invest again in a utility company.

22

Revel in Right Moments

EXPERIENCE HAS EXPANDED MY investment possibilities and my tools for dealing with change, difficulties, uncertainty, and good fortune, both in growing wealth and growing a garden.

For many years, before I planted my garden, I felt ashamed of my lawn during late fall and throughout the winter. Wet leaves littered the yard, front and back. They huddled in many places, a few under the deck after I swept them off and many in piles after raking, but before I had time to take them away. They killed life underneath them, stuck in place through the winter wetness and darkness and into spring.

I love the trees lining the edges of my property. But they produce enormous amounts of leaves. Typically, the leaves begin falling as early as July, during heavy winds, and persist until November, December even. Raking leaves, sweeping them off my driveway, and moving them from our yard to the natural area at the end of my street takes consistent effort over months.

Dealing with leaves and handling yard maintenance had not risen as priorities for much of my adult life, especially when my kids were young.

Family dinners, ball games, band concerts, visits with grandparents, and laundry were all more important.

Last year brought change. The kids had exited for grown-up endeavors. The leaves fell all at once, over three days, not three months or more. This miracle of timing happened right before rain was predicted to settle in the area for days.

The rain forecast inspired us. We had a slender amount of time to avoid a slushy pile that would haunt us during the dark months of late fall and winter. For the first time, my husband and I raked leaves—all of them. Then, we gathered them and moved them in one day, well before the end of the fall.

I considered this leaf operation a success. It arose from the positive whims of nature combined with my awareness and action.

This series of fortunate events reminded me I could not control or predict the weather in detail. I consult weather apps often but have learned forecasts do not pinpoint sunny skies at a specific moment in the future. I struggle with interpreting radar reports, as color coding and movement confuse me. Instead, I check hourly forecasts and look at the sky.

There are parallels between this swift leaf removal and buying or selling based on market happenings. I cannot control the weather or the economy, forecast rainfall or the market's direction with certainty, or predict the outcomes of business decisions made by those who run the companies in which I invest. I can learn from experience and act quickly, however, scooping up leaves or buying a favorite stock at relatively low prices when conditions look right.

There are similarities, too, between the slog of clearing leaves as they fall over several weeks and the systematic purchase of shares over time. Persistence in gathering and moving them proves as effective as the one-day effort. Likewise, the slow and steady deposits into savings and investment accounts make a difference in growing wealth, not merely the big wins when I buy shares at a historic low and watch them rise in price quickly.

Again, I set aside my thoughts about choosing one approach, quick win vs steady progress. As my strengths develop and my understanding of possibilities expand, I use multiple methods to acquire assets and produce results without daily work.

Last fall, we delighted in the quick clearing of leaves. In other years, the slog of leaf removal over time, like steady investing, was not as energizing; nevertheless, sustained efforts helped us reach our goals.

The Second Essential Takeaway

Develop sources of wealth that generate income or items you need to live without your daily involvement. Be innovative or traditional, risk taking or risk averse. Do whatever works for you. Consider how your approach affects you and the world.

The Third Essential: Protect Yourself

23

Envision Possibilities

SAFEGUARDING YOURSELF FROM SIGNIFICANT loss is the most complex of the three essentials: spending less than you earn, making money without daily work, and protecting yourself. There are more ways to lose than to grow wealth, so protection requires a multipronged approach.

One of the topics covered in my gardening class centered on protection, specifically the concoction and application of natural deer repellent. Deer often munch on garden flowers, vegetables, and fruit before humans can harvest and enjoy them. Applying this repellent, if needed, can protect from loss.

Deer roam the edges of my neighborhood, but for unknown reasons they have not eaten or spoiled my vegetables. I am prepared, however, with knowledge of how to repel them.

When cultivating my small garden, I can wait until threats emerge before dealing with them. If my plants fail to flourish, I'll be disappointed but not ruined. Rather than collecting tomatoes, zucchini, peppers, and blueberries from my yard, I can visit local farmers or the grocery store's produce section.

Growing wealth, however, requires a proactive approach. Buying insurance after an accident, checking contractors' credentials after I've paid them, and consulting with attorneys regarding provisions after I've signed a contract won't help me avoid losses from past mistakes. Setbacks can be costly. Money lost is not easily replenished.

Preserving assets so they can continue to grow requires anticipating problems and striving to prevent them or lessen their effect.

Envisioning worst-case scenarios is my jam, so protecting myself has always been at the top of my mind. I worry about losses arising from everyday problems and one-in-a-million occurrences.

"Mom, relax," one of my sons would repeatedly tell me in his teenage years.

With his encouragement, I challenged myself to recalibrate my thinking. This process has meant facing fears head-on, one at a time, plus recognizing possible rewards while dealing with dangers.

24

Identify and Manage Risks

When a risk surfaces, I notice. Next, I try to determine the likelihood of a destructive event and its potential effect on my well-being. Then I take steps to contain or prevent negative impact.

Risks seem to emerge everywhere, even with garden vegetables in the kitchen.

A few years ago, I attended a session on canning for food preservation presented by an agricultural extension agent. I was afraid of using a pressure cooker, which this kind of canning requires, but had summoned the courage to learn.

After a brief welcome, before the agent launched her presentation, a fellow participant proclaimed the danger of home canning. Someone this person knew, perhaps a friend, family member, or acquaintance, had failed to apply the proper seal on one of her canned goods. This third party then consumed the food and became dangerously ill with botulism.

This fellow student articulated my unspoken fears. I listened to the presentation but decided not to can at home. My garden had not yet come to fruition. So, maybe it was unlikely I would need to can anything from my garden anyway.

Growing, consuming, and preserving vegetables should not inspire fear. Still, I deliberated on the dangers of home canning and wondered if I could take steps to mitigate these risks.

My research revealed a mere eighteen cases of botulism reported to the CDC (Centers for Disease Control and Prevention) related to home-canned vegetables, fermented foods, and similar sources in 2018. The agency does not track or mention the number of home-canned foods preserved in the United States during this time. I will speculate that the number of bad cases represented a minuscule percentage of the total.

I appreciate warnings about hidden risks. I was aware of the potential for botulism, however, before the concerned participant hijacked the canning session.

Likewise, insurance agents may disrupt our plans for fun and adventure by talking about scary things, such as outliving our savings and catastrophic loss. Sometimes, though, they support us, offering protection and a sense of security. What's problematic is discerning the difference between being hijacked and being protected.

Further, I may consult with a professional for a specific need in one aspect of my financial life, say, health insurance or a 401(k) rollover, but get pitched a slew of unrelated products. An insurance agent may urge me to buy life, disability, and long-term care insurance policies or promote comprehensive health plans over catastrophic ones. A financial advisor may insist on reviewing my entire portfolio and updating my investments. An attorney may point out areas of risk distinct from those I had previously considered.

The agent, advisor, and attorney may have identified latent needs, uncovered only because of more urgent ones. On the other hand, they may be pushing inappropriate products. If they attempt to instill fearfulness, like the canning session participant, or the opposing extreme, inspire greed, I've considered myself hijacked.

I strive to work with professionals who show me how to identify, measure, and manage risks. They acknowledge fear and anxiety but never try to manipulate me into buying products merely to calm the emotions they've provoked.

25

Pick Protection That Works for You

SPEAKING OF HIJACKING, DID you know you can buy insurance for that? Researching travel insurance, I discovered that kidnap and ransom insurance is a thing. I soon realized I could arrange coverage for almost anything. That does not mean I *should* purchase insurance for anything and everything, only that I can.

An outsider may suppose I insure nearly everything based on my fears. I like to think I buy appropriate types and amounts of insurance.

When analyzing the kinds of coverage needed and desired, I start with legally required and contractually mandated coverage. This category includes auto insurance and homeowners insurance (when I had a mortgage).

Next, I look at coverage to protect me from significant losses. These vary with life's circumstances and stages. They may include term life insurance, homeowners insurance (even after I paid off the mortgage and the lender no longer required it), liability insurance, disability insurance, special medical coverage for overseas travel, and long-term care insurance. The likelihood of filing a claim may be relatively low, but the financial impact could be significant.

In certain cases, what has stopped me from expanding my insurance coverage was not merely the risk. What discouraged me were the costs compared to the possible benefits and the restricted conditions qualifying me for a payout.

For example, when my husband and I had young children, I investigated buying disability insurance in addition to employer-sponsored coverage. The policy I reviewed paid only if either of us could not perform any kind of work, which seemed unlikely given the broad definition of work and the availability of supportive technology. Premiums ran thousands of dollars every year.

What I had examined was most likely considered any-occupation disability insurance, which is less expensive than an own-occupation policy—but also not as helpful. If either of us worked high-paying specialty jobs, such as neurosurgery or jet piloting, I would have bought own-occupation insurance. But we held office jobs, so I didn't buy this insurance. (Later, I became more aware of neurological diseases that strike and impair younger people and may have purchased a policy if I knew then what I know now.)

Despite my reasonable approach to most insurance-related situations, I will not claim to be entirely rational in all my insurance decisions. For example, I purchased insurance on new mobile phones for the family when my sons were teenagers. This move averted distress associated with replacing or repairing phones in addition to covering the financial loss.

I've also arranged for an earthquake rider on my homeowners insurance. Again, I am uncertain of its value. But the price is reasonable, and the coverage gives me peace of mind.

Buying insurance is a standard, reasonable solution for mitigating risk. An alternative is self-insuring for specific dangers. To bring about this arrangement, I set aside money for a potential loss rather than send money to an insurance company. The upside is there are no formal claims; I simply withdraw the funds designated for repair or restoration, no questions asked (of myself!). The downside is I may not be able to save enough to cover a loss, especially if it happens early in the self-insurance process—before I accumulate enough savings for this purpose. Still, this approach remains an option, especially if I cannot purchase a policy with acceptable terms.

Further, self-insurance does not have to be all or nothing. I can partially insure myself by asking my agent for a high deductible, having a lengthy self-coverage period before insurance kicks in, or somehow limiting the coverage.

I see danger everywhere, including the phones in the pockets of my teenage sons (when they were younger) and fault lines in the mountains of North Carolina. A small amount each year is dedicated to dealing with these fears. In general, though, I weigh the odds and calculate the cost of losses, scrutinize the probability and amounts of insurance payouts, and aim to buy insurance only when it matters.

26

Set Boundaries

BEYOND TRADITIONAL PROTECTION MEASURES like insurance, I started noticing the need to set boundaries. This practice emerged as an essential technique for protecting myself. When I consider boundaries, I think of literal ones.

Many years ago, a neighbor may have believed he was protecting his boundary but overstepped mine instead. He warned against trespassing by nailing a sign onto a tree at the entrance of a neighborhood yard waste depository. I had been told that this wooded area had been left natural by the developer, who permitted neighbors to put their leaves, grass clippings, and tree limbs there.

Over the years, yard waste etiquette had evolved, specifying yard debris placement and allowing newer homeowners like my husband and me to add our stuff to the ever-growing and ever-decomposing pile. The larger natural area that encircled the mound bordered our properties, but the trimmings were far from the property lines.

My take was that this arrangement preserved everyone's rights. It also allowed us to avoid paying for yard waste pickup and suffocating our lawn grass while waiting for the city to gather leaves and other debris.

The natural area where the guy installed the sign was not his property. The sign caused a brief hubbub. Then someone took it down.

I will go out on a limb and say my neighbor had boundary issues.

Most of the people I deal with in my work, whether clients or colleagues, and in the community, whether neighbors or cycling group members, respect boundaries, both their own and mine, whether property lines or personal finance. On rare occasions, I encounter a person who does not grasp the meaning of drawn lines or oversteps them for personal benefit or a power play.

You may know someone who doesn't see or respect boundaries. They might plan an activity for the group and cancel at the last minute or come up short when the bill comes due. They take their time with rent payments, often when the landlord is a family member or friend. They ask for and receive favors yet balk at returning them.

That is not to say regular, boundary-abiding people never need anything.

For example, a friend's younger relative, whom I will call Ken, moved to my town and needed a favor. My friend asked if I could be a resource for him, and I agreed.

Ken asked me to be a reference and cosigner for his utility bill. It was an unusual request. However, my friend was the definition of the salt of the earth, so I agreed, in general, and then spoke with the local utility representative about the details.

"How much would I be on the hook for if Ken doesn't pay?" I asked.

The answer was a hundred dollars, maximum. I also discovered I would be the backup payer for six months until Ken established his credit with the company. For this small amount, in the short term, I could help him arrange for electricity. This cost was worth the risk.

When my friend heard how I'd agreed to help her relative, she seemed flabbergasted.

"I can't believe Ken asked you to do this. That's not what I had in mind when I gave him your name," she said.

She reacted as I expected, which was one of the reasons I signed on, knowing she would cover for me if needed. Ken may have unwittingly crossed a boundary, but I felt glad to help. My dad cosigned for my car loan when I accepted my first job in a city without public transportation, so I understood this need for someone else's help. I gather that all went well with Ken and his utility bill, as I never had to shell out any money on his behalf.

I have known people well beyond the start-up phase of life who have sought help again and again. They may ask me to cosign a loan, invest in a business, or tap cash reserves or professional time on their behalf. I put up my guard when the behavior mimics my colorful neighbor with his sign and that of those who are cavalier with other people's property, whether land, creditworthiness, time, or cash. I must set and enforce my boundaries to protect myself.

27

Recognize Blind Spots

I CONSIDER MYSELF KIND yet discerning, able to recognize potential threats, like my signposting neighbor, while knowing when to dismiss concerns, like when I vouched for my friend's cousin.

An incident at a hotel's breakfast bar revealed a blind spot. I should have been waving a caution flag in front of my son, but issuing a warning never occurred to me.

As my husband and son slept in our hotel outside a military base in southern Georgia, I had wandered downstairs to start the day. My son was scheduled to receive his commission as a military officer in a few hours.

This whole military family thing signified a new phase of life, so I was unsure what to expect. Getting going as early as possible usually helps with anything new, so there I was.

I drank coffee, feeling alone in the crowded breakfast room. Then I saw a woman with a Carolina Hornets shirt, smiled at her, and welcomed her to join me. I prefer college basketball over professional basketball, but I sensed we might have something to talk about since she likely hailed from my home state.

We did. Or should I say: did we ever! Mainly, though, I listened.

She had spent years as a military wife and mom. Like my son, her nephew would soon receive commissioning as an officer. My breakfast companions (her grown daughter was with her) had traveled to celebrate this accomplishment.

I told them about my son; they told me about their relative. Then my son texted, asked to join me, and appeared.

My new friend and her daughter took one look at my son and said, "He's so handsome" and "We need to talk to him."

Back home, before his departure for training, my husband, son, and I watched *An Officer and a Gentleman*, a movie about the interactions between locals and aspiring aviators being trained at a nearby naval installation. But we never discussed the movie and its implications for all freshly commissioned military officers, not just the pilots featured on-screen.

My friends wasted no time. The daughter pulled him aside. From what I gathered, she warned him to protect himself. She likely told him not to be hoodwinked by a woman who might be eager to secure his financial support at a high cost to him. Default to distrust was the message.

I could not believe I had missed this threat. I thought of my son as my child, not the source of security for a wily person. I felt fortunate to have met these women, not only for their camaraderie but also for their voices of experience. I sensed these concerns had been discussed among my son's fellow officer candidates. But my breakfast buddies spoke with authority directly to him.

This encounter reminded me that if I do not recognize a family member as a possible mark, others may be unlikely to see themselves or those close to them as one either.

There are certain times and situations when a family member, friend, or I may be vulnerable. These include when someone expects or receives a windfall, such as inheritances or proceeds from a business deal; holds a high-status and high-paying job or one with extraordinary benefits; receives money from a trust fund; becomes divorced; grieves the death of a spouse; and ages, especially if other people know this person lives alone and struggles to make sound financial decisions.

I do not want to become paranoid. But it makes sense to be attuned to the possibility that someone else may want to profit from a relationship. Protecting myself means heightened awareness and consulting with professionals before making significant moves involving other people.

28

Get Professional Help

GETTING PROFESSIONAL HELP MAY mean meeting with a financial advisor, tax accountant, counselor, insurance agent, or attorney who can advise on protecting myself and my family. It may also involve hiring an expert to handle daunting or dangerous tasks such as cutting down trees or staking a party tent.

During the pandemic, my sisters and I decided to throw a party to celebrate my dad's birthday. The guest list consisted of his children (my sisters and me), grandchildren, great-grandchildren, and assorted spouses.

Putting a party together is never easy. Add protecting ourselves from a potentially deadly virus, guests traveling from out of town, and a pending hurricane, and things became complicated.

My oldest sister planned to host the event in her backyard, where we could eat outside, spread out, and remove masks. We wanted to take precautions and help our dad (and us) stay well. Then we heard a weather forecast of an 80 percent chance of rain before, during, and after the party. My sister's house was not in danger of being ripped away by hurricane-force winds, as she lives far inland. But the rain could cause flash floods and drench the party.

I researched tents, both buying and renting. Because I could reuse the tent for parties at my house, I looked at buying, a clever solution to the pandemic-gathering dilemma. I liked how the numbers worked out on a per-use basis. However, no large tents were available for purchase, so renting was our only option.

My sisters and I texted to determine the proper course of action. Change the date? No way. Hope for sunshine? Yes. Rent the tent anyway? Absolutely.

The bill for the tent rental seemed high, nearly twice the cost of the food. Upon seeing the tent installed, I was impressed with its sturdiness and excellent staking. Not a string or stake dangled within the tent's interior. Outside, the enormous stakes grounding the tent appeared immovable. Nothing would stop this party.

A week later, I spoke about the get-together and tent rental with a friend, who manages an event venue. Her weekend involved a wedding and preparation for various weather scenarios, including predicted rain.

I was surprised when she told me the tent's price was excellent.

"You know," she said, "if someone tripped on the rope holding the stake, you'd be responsible for medical bills arising from the fall. Let the vendor handle it, and they'd be on the hook for any problems."

One of the reasons for the large bill came into focus.

Professional help can be costly, but expert guidance can help save a special event and accelerate learning curves. Even after taking the gardening class, I consulted with a professional when I wanted someone to help me with persistent weeds and expand my growing capacity to include a small fruit orchard. As a result, I discovered ways to protect my plants from intruders and disease.

Nothing about our family causes me to believe one member would sue another. However, I know firsthand that insurance companies take measures to collect medical bills. I have filled out more than one insurance form affirming my fault (and no one else's!) for a quirky accident.

I refuse to worry about parties I host. But I will start feeling happier about paying professionals to work for me.

29

Consider Outside Influences

As a young investor, wife, and mom, I focused on protecting my family and myself from losses associated with personal decisions and individual threats, such as the impact of an illness or a house fire. I wasn't sure how to deal with broader concerns, such as economic turmoil and stock market slumps.

I graduated from college and searched for my first real job during the economic recession of the early 1980s. I didn't fully appreciate the context of my challenges at the time and tended to blame myself rather than difficult circumstances—despite knowing others were struggling as well. Ultimately, I landed a job in a small town, where I met my husband, who had taken an entry-level position with a retail chain after nearly a year of job searching. Eventually, we could save, invest, and take advantage of his employer's stock program.

Five years after my graduation, in October 1987, my husband and I experienced a sharp decline in the value of our stock market holdings, particularly the shares of his employer's stock, on the day now known as Black Monday. At the time, well before the advent of digital dashboards,

I didn't appreciate the loss (on paper). I sensed our finances had time to recover as we continued to acquire shares of desirable companies and funds.

As I grew wealth in the early days, I seemed to suffer *and* benefit from economic mayhem. Sure, my account balances fell in value during economic blips and crises. But I was able to acquire new shares at bargain prices as long as I earned income and maintained my investing habit.

The more I acquired, though, the more I wanted and needed to protect what I owned. Preserving wealth brought a different sort of challenge.

I learned that changing, uncertain, and difficult conditions are givens, so it's logical to pay attention to what's going on in the world, no matter my stage of life.

As a gardener, I stay alert to ground temperature, frost warnings, and rain forecasts. I often plan and adjust my activities accordingly. For example, I wait until the ground is warmed before sowing seeds for an early summer harvest, bring my potted lemon tree inside when frost is imminent, and often plant just before rain, to facilitate seed germination.

Likewise, as a wealth grower, I notice economic and business happenings and consider how I might respond to save money, invest more fruitfully, protect myself, and help others. However, I have struggled with the specifics of how to act during challenging times.

Several years ago, a friend said she saw a crisis looming but could not stop it. Her employer, a major bank, was making bad credit decisions. These decisions reflected intention, not errors in subjective judgment. Her impression was that bank officials were chasing short-term profits to the detriment of customers and the bank itself.

The bank was issuing mortgage loans requiring minimal or no documentation of the borrower's repayment ability. It also was allowing borrowers to pick their payment amounts, which may not have covered interest charges or facilitated the paydown of loan principal.

This kind of mortgage seemed foreign to me. The bank had scrutinized us closely when my husband and I took out our first mortgage loan. Because we had paid off two car loans several weeks before finalizing the mortgage deal, we had to explain why our cash holdings had increased dramatically. Paying off the debt freed cash from our paychecks and allowed us to divert extra money to build our bank balances. Our prudence created suspicion!

Further, a non-amortizing loan wasn't yet in my vocabulary. I loved creating mortgage amortization schedules and reveled in checking my formulas by verifying that the remaining balance at the end of a fifteen-year and thirty-year mortgage equaled zero at fifteen and thirty years, respectively. The idea that payments would not pay off a loan did not compute.

Still, how could bad decisions by borrowers and lenders hundreds of miles away affect my financial situation? After a few borrowers defaulted and the homes were repossessed, wouldn't the bank absorb the losses?

It was not merely lax lending policies that created the subprime financial crisis, later known as the Great Recession. Missteps multiplied.

Another contributor to the catastrophe was the packaging (a.k.a. securitization) of questionable high-risk loans with moderate and high-quality mortgages, then rated as high quality all-around and sold as safe investments to financial institutions and large investors. Credit rating agencies falsely graded these securities as high quality, dispensing with their sole purpose in life—to let institutional investors know which investments carried high risks and which did not.

While borrowers enjoyed their new homes and brokers raked in their commissions, mortgage packages were bought and sold. Further, bankers placed bets on the future values of these bundles through complicated financial arrangements.

These deals multiplied the potential payoffs while also making possible deep losses. Eventually, defaults on mortgage loans affected not only individual borrowers but also the entire financial system.

Rather than explore the timeline of the financial system's near breakdown or whether the federal government should have rescued financial institutions from failure, I will relate how I felt at the time.

I was scared.

I was also annoyed. The financial caution I had practiced all those years appeared fruitless. Other people's recklessness had a more significant influence on my financial status than my diligence!

This crisis affected the pillars of financial stability: the stock market, the housing market, and the jobs market. This situation overturned my previous understanding of how things worked: A crisis in one area would be offset by opportunities in another.

Financial experts describe this stable arrangement as uncorrelated risk. Invest in stocks, bonds, and real estate, while running your business or working a job, and when one fails, the other endures to sustain you. This trifecta of support works, except when it does not. This time, the whole system came tumbling down.

Before the 2008–09 crisis, I'd never fully trusted financial institutions. But I didn't envision they'd bring themselves down *and* ask for government handouts—while handing out bonuses to their top executives!

I was never in danger of losing my home. I had enough in investments to pay off the remainder of the mortgage. But the value of my stock holdings fell. If I made withdrawals when the market was down, that would erode future growth more than ever. I feared what might become of the sturdiness of my financial plans.

Here's where the pitfall of having a fifteen-year mortgage and paying extra on the principal came to light. At this point, during the Great Recession, we had not yet paid off the mortgage and still had the fixed expenses associated with these monthly payments. Instead of shoring up cash reserves in a bank account, I had applied extra money to paying down the mortgage. Unfortunately, there was no simple, fast way to extract cash from this asset, our home, and I didn't want to borrow money using home equity. Regarding fixed expenses and cash flow, being close to paying off the mortgage equated with being years away.

My freelance work had slowed, and my husband's employer suffered as credit tightened, foreclosures mounted, jobs disappeared, and stock prices fell.

During this time, Bernie Madoff was convicted of defrauding investors. A former chairman of Nasdaq, Madoff cheated people who had trusted him with their money. An element of this case intrigued me. Madoff's firm had issued client statements indicating steady annual growth of about 10 percent, rather than showing fluctuations consistent with the broader market. Of course, these statements were fraudulent, but why hadn't more of Madoff's clients suspected something so unlikely as steady, unwavering growth, year after year, even as the market's performance fluctuated?

Never again would I trust linear growth.

Significant setbacks, then, must be expected. These are more than late frosts or spotty rainfall for a season. They're persistent droughts that deprive plants of water needed to flourish and high temperatures that thwart the pollination of tomato plants. They're also problems I've yet to experience but have been warned about, like pests damaging my newly planted peach trees and deer munching on apples before I harvest them.

My diligence as a gardener would need to extend beyond the initial sprouting stages to one of protecting growth and preserving my harvests.

Whether growing tomatoes or growing wealth, there were outside influences to consider. During various economic setbacks, I began to grasp that other people—consumers, public-policy decision makers, institutional investors, and individual investors like me—influence my finances, often in unexpected and undeserved ways. For much of my life, my toolbox had been limited to exercising greater frugality, hoping for a brighter future, and concentrating on what I could control. I had more to learn.

30

Prepare for Downturns

While reading a personal finance book, I encountered a term encapsulating a wealth protection problem I had struggled to articulate: sequence-of-returns risk. Before that moment, I believed my failure to mitigate this peril was a personal flaw.

Sequence-of-returns risk is the danger that a bad year in the stock market, say a decline of 30 percent, occurs when you must sell investments to pay for a significant expense, such as retirement. Selling shares low diminishes the wealth base from which returns are earned for the rest of a person's retired life.

I knew year-over-year investment returns varied from the average, delivering more than expected in many years and dropping worse than feared in others. As I grew wealth, these swings benefited me, making me feel thankful (and intelligent) during growth periods and allowing me to acquire shares at lower prices during declines.

What I did not consider was the emotional and financial impact of market drops when I needed to sell and I could not take advantage of lower prices as a buyer.

The math is simple but not obvious.

For example, suppose I held $100,000 in investments earmarked for college tuition and earned a 10 percent average annual return. In that case, I could withdraw $10,000 each year to contribute to a child's college bill in perpetuity and maintain the principal indefinitely. However, if returns turned negative, say -20 percent for two years in a row, and then rebounded to +40 percent for the subsequent two years and +10 percent after that (an average of 10 percent), I would deplete my investment base to about $3,500 in fifteen years.

Averages are helpful for planning but returns in real life are experienced in random order. Sequences matter.

Starting in my twenties, I focused on growing wealth, a challenging task itself. Fortunately, contemplating long time horizons came naturally to me. When markets fell, I knew they would rise again.

It did not occur to me how different managing and preserving wealth would be compared to accumulating wealth. Suddenly, the short term clashed with the long term in ways I had not anticipated. Withdrawing money in down markets made me feel uneasy and unsure of myself. At first, I could only embrace frugality more tightly as I awaited the next upturn.

What shifted for me was the naming of the risk. I was able to acknowledge that my discomfort came not from my imagination but rather from an investment danger to be confronted. No longer lurking in the shadows, sequence-of-returns risk could be battled with new strategies.

A couple of basic approaches came to mind. One was to increase my cash position. This money could cover my essential bills, allowing me to avoid selling when prices dropped during economic crises.

Another solution was to continue working at a paid job or self-owned business (or start a business as a retirement project). A complementary approach would be to develop income streams by acquiring assets that produce cash without being liquidated. Examples included stocks that pay dividends and real estate that generates rental income.

Likewise, as a gardener, I can anticipate and prepare for years when my garden won't yield much. I freeze fruits and vegetables from my bounty and then consume them during these times. I might also consider growing vegetables year-round rather than planting a summer garden only and setting aside funds to spend with farmers who sell produce when my garden isn't productive.

Learning to garden was a massive step for me, but just the beginning. If I'd like to enjoy produce for many years, there's more to learn and do.

The biggest gain from naming the risk was not monetary. Realizing why fortifying my financial position differed from amassing wealth buoyed my courage to continue to learn.

This insight inspired me to keep more cash on hand and sharpen my investing skills. Rather than merely acquiring great companies, I learned how to estimate their values. I adopted a discounted cash flow method that I read about in *The Five Rules for Successful Stock Investing: Morningstar's Guide to Building Wealth and Winning in the Market* by Pat Dorsey. This technique involves projecting a company's cash flow in the future and determining its value in the present. I could then compare the dollar amount of this value to a stock's current price. If the going price exceeded its worth, I wouldn't invest in the company at that time.

This approach did not protect me from all downturns. It helped me, however, to avoid buying shares at extraordinarily high prices, which tended to fall in subsequent months or stagnate as inherent values slowly caught up with market prices.

I realized that embedded in the financial recommendations of advisors and media experts are reasonable yet undisclosed assumptions regarding their audience's needs. Guidance tends to be skewed toward building wealth or maintaining wealth, rarely both. Financial journalists may tilt toward building wealth without regard for controlling losses. Advice from traditional advisors tends to focus on preserving wealth, slanted toward averting losses rather than growing account values.

Depending on an investor's timeline and other factors, such as the capacity to lose money without suffering, this sequencing problem could be overmanaged at the risk of not fully participating in market growth or buying pricey services as a hedge. Ironically, then, protecting myself aggressively could also be risky.

I intend to keep learning and hone my practical expertise to manage sequence-of-returns and similar money perils.

Difficult circumstances beyond my control alarm me. However, world happenings also remind me to enjoy the present moment even as I deal with outside influences. Identifying opportunities for loss is easy. What's tricky is practicing awareness and vigilance while living joyfully and generously.

The Third Essential Takeaway

PROTECTING YOURSELF, YOUR GARDEN, and your wealth requires anticipating and dealing with potential problems. This process necessitates being aware of your circumstances, consulting with professionals, and continually learning. Even as you look ahead to anticipate and deal with perils, experience joy in the moment.

The Connections: Grow Wealth like You Garden

31

Sow Seeds

When I started my garden, soon after taking the class with the welcoming instructor, I decided to grow vegetables from seeds. My teacher had suggested this approach could work.

Before attending and soaking up the lessons from the class, I had tried to start a garden with small plants called seedlings. I failed. Or rather, the plants died. Or the store where I purchased them failed me. Anyway, nothing grew.

I decided to try again with seeds, equipped with knowledge from my class and a belief that I could succeed. My first venture, in which I attempted to grow ground cover with wildflower seeds, had failed. But now I knew a possible reason why: No sun was available to nurture the seeds' growth.

I also began to suspect that certain seeds were superior to others. Instead of blaming my ineptitude for the seeds' failure to sprout, I looked outside of myself and decided to find higher quality sources, or at least ones suitable for my purposes.

About the time of my class, I became acquainted with a source for seeds through my work as a freelance writer. The owner of a gardening company specializing in seed-of-the-month subscriptions responded to a media query about price discounts on Small Business Saturday®. That year, readers with certain plastic cards could score a triple win: support small business owners, snag deals, and qualify for a card statement credit.

Not only did I write about the seed seller, but I also bought a subscription. My seeds arrived in my mailbox with basic instructions on the packet.

So far, my gardening technique has involved placing seeds at the depth, spacing, and soil temperature specified on the packet. When possible, I plant before forecasted rain appears. If rain does not occur, I water the soil gently.

Seed packets also contain instructions about the timing of starting seeds indoors. Generally, I ignore these sections.

By planting seeds directly into the soil, I skip either buying plants from a gardening supply store or coddling my seeds inside to coax them to sprout and then replanting them. Those techniques seem tiring and traumatic, both for me and the would-be vegetables, grains, and herbs.

Since plants need nutrients from the soil and sunlight, it makes sense to me to plant the seeds outdoors in the garden from the start.

My lingering doubt is the biggest problem I've had with the seeds. I tend to plant too many seeds too close together, as I'm skeptical they will all grow. More plants appear than I expect, and then they compete for nutrients. After seeing what takes root and sprouts, I could remove extras—a process called thinning. But I'm not fond of yanking out green things, so I let everything grow.

My garden is not perfect. My approach, however, is simple, straightforward, and accessible.

When I mention to friends who garden that I grow vegetables from seeds, they are amazed at my growing prowess. They view me as a gardening prodigy, who coaxes life from inanimate objects.

My gardening follows a technique, not one I invented but one I've merely adopted for its ease and effectiveness. In addition, it allows me to leverage nature instead of trying to outsmart it.

I apply a similar method to investing, doing what seems the simplest and capitalizing on my strengths. My investments consist primarily of shares of specific businesses, that is, individual stocks. Except in accounts with limited choices, such as 401(k)s and HSAs, I avoid investing in ETFs and mutual funds. I prefer choosing the companies I own and understanding their intrinsic values relative to prices.

A fundamental approach informs my decisions, involving cash flow projections and evaluations of balance sheets of individual companies. It is not new or innovative but simply a framework I adopted by reading books like *The Intelligent Investor* by Benjamin Graham and *The Five Rules for Successful Stock Investing*, then applying my understanding of business, finance, and accounting.

Friends and acquaintances seem amazed to learn that I buy individual stocks, just as they are astounded at my ability to grow vegetables from seeds. I do what makes sense to me.

32

Let It Grow

I PLANTED MY FIRST garden by following instructions from my teacher and the seed packet. I readied an area of land with good soil and sunlight. I sowed seeds, from the seed-of-the-month subscription, that included amaranth.

I had no idea what amaranth was. My lack of knowledge did not hinder me.

My plants emerged from the soil. They grew, especially the amaranth, which became tall and dwarfed me. When I inspected my garden, I saw new life growing. My elegant amaranth thrilled me.

I felt pride at a plant grown and skill mastered. Why hadn't I planted seeds before?

Have you ever invested a small amount and then reaped a great reward almost immediately?

33

Harvest the Returns

GROWING AMARANTH WAS EASY. Turning the plant into food was not. I forgot to consider harvesting, processing, and the multitude of steps from growing to consuming.

My background in gardening and harvesting was limited. As a child, and later as an adult with my children, I gathered strawberries, cherries, and blueberries from pick-your-own farms. I discerned the ripeness of fruits, judging from their textures, tastes, and gentle releases from their vines. I bought fresh vegetables from farmers or stood by my parents' sides as they did. I capped strawberries, pitted cherries, snapped beans, and shucked corn.

Unlike my work with those familiar fruits and vegetables, I had no idea what to do with amaranth. I researched the specifics of its consumption. From what I could tell, by the time I became aware of the need to harvest, the time to pick and consume its greenery had passed. Its seeds, however, were available. They represented organic gold, free of gluten and a source of healthy protein when appropriately processed.

Suggested steps included cutting, drying, and separating seeds from the plant. First, I cut and gathered its tall stalks and placed them on my kitchen table and nearby spaces. Next, I began the process of drying, which I then determined to be ambiguous in its doneness. After a week of amaranth dominating my kitchen and sunroom, I abandoned the project.

Buying ready-to-eat amaranth at the grocery store seemed more manageable than spending weeks transforming my amaranth from a towering plant to real food.

The awareness that not only do gardeners grow things but they also pick and process them startled me. Though thrilled at my early growing success, I did not factor in the time, effort, and expertise that turning my harvest into easily consumed food would take.

The resources required to create consumables from plants reminded me of turning assets into spending money.

Just as the planting to harvesting time for vegetables varies, investments produce income at varying schedules. Savings accounts might pay interest monthly, for example. Certain stocks pay dividends quarterly; some generate cash only when sold. Businesses and rental properties may yield income monthly and produce money when sold.

How fast I can turn investments into cash, known as liquidity, differs from one type to another. Money in a savings account can be withdrawn quickly. Stocks listed on the NYSE (New York Stock Exchange) or Nasdaq may sell in minutes and settle in accounts within a few days. Real estate may sell in days or weeks. Investments in private equity and businesses may take years to redeem.

Getting started may be effortless. Yet turning an investment or plant into a consumable may be more difficult than anticipated.

After cultivating amaranth, I grew more vegetables, such as zucchini and tomatoes. As it turns out, amaranth was the most challenging to transform into food. The zucchinis required effort to roast, sauté, or steam for a meal, though they could be eaten raw. The tomatoes were the easiest. I picked them off the vine, then sliced or cut them to size for use in a sandwich, salad, or side dish. They could also be frozen whole and later boiled to release their tough skin, then included in soups and chilis.

Someone who adheres to a gluten-free diet may love to grow amaranth; others may revel in abundant zucchini or crave homegrown tomatoes. Someone may love the tangible aspect of real estate, plus excel at renovations and renter relationships; I enjoy the ease of owning and managing a portfolio consisting mainly of stocks and cash.

There is no right or wrong seed to sow. But it makes sense to ponder personal preferences and weigh the time, patience, and other resources to bring plants and investments to fruition.

34

Consider the Costs

JUST AS THERE'S TIME and effort required to convert garden plants into consumables and investment assets into cash, these conversions carry various costs. In my garden, these costs may be associated with picking, processing, and storing produce.

Likewise, there may be charges for acquiring, holding, and selling investments, such as management fees on mutual funds; operating expenses and capital expenditures for businesses; property taxes, insurance, and upkeep costs on real estate properties; and transaction fees paid to brokers, attorneys, and other professionals. Expenses include income taxes, such as ordinary income taxes on interest income, and capital gains taxes on the sale of equity investments, such as stocks and stakes in businesses.

When I first contemplated growing wealth, I never considered the impact of taxes. That came later. Another teacher planted the seed to pay attention.

"Paying more income tax than required is a sin," my instructor at the community college said.

I took a taxation course to learn how to file my taxes, just as I signed up for the gardening class to expand my practical knowledge.

Since then, I have done my darnedest not to sin when doing my taxes, claiming deductions and credits, and eventually learning to plan my income and adjustments such as credits and itemizations.

Paying attention to numbers and money came naturally to me. Taking notice of taxes was an acquired habit.

Attending to the tax code did not improve my cash flow or influence my decisions at the start of my career. Money was withheld from my paycheck throughout the year. Later, a day of reckoning came when I determined my tax liability. I calculated the payment due or refund from the IRS or state department of revenue. We settled accounts each year, and then we started over again.

At my first real job, I contributed to my 401(k), reducing my taxable income. Eager to start saving for retirement, I funded the account for reasons unrelated to taxes. The tax break was a bonus, not part of a grand strategy.

(At the time, Roth IRAs and Roth 401(k)s did not exist. Funds in these accounts hold the promise of no taxes later in life, a sweet deal in retirement.)

Strategizing for taxes started when excitement emerged about cafeteria-style benefits at work. These plans capitalized on a specific section

(125) of the tax law. When a company offers a menu of employee benefits, these costs could be deducted from income, both for the employer and its employees.

People hoped this tax rule would prompt the expansion of benefits. I do not remember the addition of employment perks, such as discounted gym memberships. Eventually, the mania regarding tax reduction possibilities subsided. Nevertheless, I enjoyed lower taxable income for paying my share of health insurance premiums as a paycheck deduction. Section 125 of the IRS code sounded sexier in theory than it was in reality. It did, however, spark the idea of looking for tax savings.

Besides my instructor's admonition, what ignited my curiosity about income taxes arose from a tax bill for mutual funds. I owed taxes for this investment during a year when its value plummeted while I continued holding shares. As a result, not only did the value of my shares fall, but the investment did not generate the cash to pay these taxes.

The rules about taxes on mutual funds are quirky. Capital gains on investments held within the fund are passed to shareholders, even if individual investors do not sell shares.

The situation reminded me of my business law class in college. A solid B+ student, I still came close to failing this class. Despite my diligence in attending class and studying the material, my test scores were dismal. For a mysterious reason, the study habits that had sustained me throughout my academic life were, abruptly, inadequate.

I attended a tutoring session where a few words from the teaching assistant illuminated my problem. I realized I did not need to scrutinize the textbook. Instead, I needed to understand that the law was distinct from what I believed was logical and ethical. Mastering business law involved learning and applying the rules, not reasoning through various situations. With this epiphany and no additional studying, I aced the final exam.

Tax code fell within the category of business law, and I wanted to ace my taxes every year.

I have not yet mastered the law or taxes, as the rules and my situation keep changing. Still, I pay attention to subtleties after the mutual funds debacle. I am attuned to scenarios where I could owe more taxes than expected or pay less because of the money moves I make.

Some may argue saving money on taxes or strategizing to save money in taxes is a rich person's game. Others may believe making tax-saving moves signifies foolishness, leading to actions against one's self-interest.

I have encountered professionals who seem aggressive in dissuading their clients, friends, acquaintances, and readers from pursuing tax planning. I may be overly sensitive to managing cash flow but find such discouragement manipulative.

Here is what I believe: Knowledge is power.

Investing and understanding the tax code can empower the powerless and marginalized. People who do not have the educational pedigrees, life circumstances, family support, and specific ambitions to land and hold high-paying jobs can still invest and do well. Sure, they can also earn money from side gigs to fortify their financial positions, but these activities may detract from other priorities.

It is worth knowing that relatively low income and long-term holding of investments could result in zero dollars owed in capital gains taxes. In contrast, revenue from a side hustle is likely to generate taxes.

Just because I envision aspects of my future financial state (including my tax liability) does not make me greedy or foolish. Understanding taxes may result in positive moves, like buying and holding an investment for the favorable tax treatment of capital gains or giving to charity more than usual to boost itemized deductions.

I want to know what triggers a taxable event, what tiers of income allow or prevent me from claiming deductions and credits, and what simple actions I can take to reduce my taxes.

Likewise, when I plant seeds for my garden, I consider the difficulty of tending the plants and the potential payoff compared to the quality and cost of alternatives available from my local farmers, farmers markets, and grocery stores. I also factor in the labor involved in harvesting, preparing, and storing my excess vegetables, herbs, and fruit.

Gardening is a hobby. I do not approach growing green things by projecting their potential returns on investment. Still, I do not ignore the labor involved, just as I will not stop looking at the tax implications of my financial decisions.

35

Deal with Distractions

FOR SOME, PAYING ATTENTION to taxes distracts from growing wealth. Likewise, weeds may interfere with nurturing a garden. I embrace the paradox that taxes and weeds represent both diversions and items worthy of attention.

No matter my views, proper weeding was a skill to sharpen in my quest to become a productive gardener.

First, I needed to recognize weeds. During my inaugural gardening season, my husband believed runner greenery could be a green bean plant. I wasn't so sure. But since he had helped with his parents' garden (a few hours' drive away, located on a family farm his dad had acquired from his mother's estate) and I had no experience, I decided to wait and see if it would yield vegetables or show itself as a pesky weed.

For many gardeners, differentiating between a weed and a sowed vegetable is a cinch. Many maintain records of what they planted and where. I tried to keep good notes but was not confident in my documentation or recollection. My uncertainty was partly due to my missing the mark in planting neat rows—a concept I understood in theory, but which eluded me in its execution. My plantings look like jumbles of growth.

Likewise, some people smooth their dollar bills and order them in their wallets based on denomination, often with ones on top and twenties in the back. Meanwhile, I cram crumpled currency in purse compartments and delight in whatever cash I can fish out. I admire neatness in other people but know that smoothed or crumpled, the paper money spends the same. In gardens, though, orderliness may help with plant identification.

For the runner plant, I installed a gardening app to identify plants based on images I captured on my phone's camera. I snapped and uploaded a photo, then received multiple suggestions of its identity. None seemed correct based on growing regions, seasons, and descriptions.

I decided to err in favor of letting green things grow rather than plucking a thriving plant. By the end of summer, the runners my husband supposed could be beans revealed themselves as weeds—malicious ones. They choked the growth of my vegetables.

Not perceiving the difference between healthy veggies and destructive plants frustrated me. However, when these weeds reappeared in subsequent years, I removed them swiftly.

Both in gardening and growing wealth, technology may accelerate the learning curve. It may help me deal with distractions. But apps will never replace hands-on experience.

36

Reflect and Refine

One of my gardening goals is to find an effective weed elimination strategy that benefits my garden and me.

Likewise, as I gained financial footing in my twenties, I realized that a reasonable money goal was to develop a giving plan benefiting my community and me. My beliefs on weeding and giving converged in this area. Small, concentrated efforts proved worthwhile, but a more significant impact was possible and more attainable with forethought.

My plan entailed examining personal and family finances. It also necessitated prioritization, reflection, and rejiggering.

I controlled major fixed expenses for line items like housing, transportation, and health care premiums intuitively. My philosophies of borrowing less than banks allowed and scrutinizing details benefited my bank accounts. Living in areas with affordable housing helped.

More challenging was controlling the smaller purchases, which added up over time. Lattes didn't interfere with my wealth building, as coffee menus confuse me. Fashion trends escape me, so shopping excursions for fun rarely caused a shortfall. Restaurant dinners and gear for hobbies emerged as the culprits derailing my discretionary budget.

Charitable giving offered a way to exercise control. Achieving a higher level of giving centered on changing habits and strategizing my spending, not simply striving to become more generous.

At the risk of sounding anti-altruistic, I learned that budgeting for giving benefited my financial discipline. It prompted me to look at what I valued and match what I claimed to believe with my spending. At first, this process seemed like a one-time thing.

Now I see that aligning my finances with my values, especially around charitable giving, persists as a lifetime gig—one that involves evaluating and rethinking finances and priorities at various life stages.

Whenever I wander outside and survey my plants, I mull over the best way to deal with weeds. Tending daily to my garden works, as does micromanaging my finances. However, I want easier maintenance for both.

I'm still experimenting with techniques, including one that involves the placement of landscape fabric over dirt. This method allows water to enter the ground but blocks weeds from emerging and growing so tall they block the sun and steal nutrients from my vegetables and fruits.

Each season and year, I gain fresh insights and a deeper understanding of what's effective in reaching my goals. I still make mistakes, generally new ones, not the same old ones. Progress happens by applying experience, making brand-new mistakes, and continually learning.

In my garden now, I know those runners as weeds and pull them as soon as they appear. Weed recognition represents a triumph, like prioritizing my spending to create room for giving. Both require continual effort as new kinds of weeds and temptations to squander surface.

37

Enjoy the Bounty

My amaranth stalks heralded my ability to grow thriving plants from seeds.

Later in my first gardening season, I grew peppers, loads of them. The following summer, I brought in an overflow of homegrown tomatoes, signaling my status as a legitimate gardener in the southeastern United States. Last year, my zucchini plants took over my garden and the surrounding yard with shoots of yellow blooms, soon replaced with the fruit of nature's labor. I also grew cilantro and parsley, which survived multiple touches of frost and stayed green even in winter.

I never imagined I would need to deal with overwhelming amounts of vegetables. I was not an expert gardener or even a good one. I believed it would be a fluke if my peppers grew at all or my tomatoes or zucchini. Instead, they flourished, not all at once but in successive seasons.

I dealt with the bounty by adopting a seasonal mindset. If vegetables showed up in my garden, they appeared at dinner, lunch, and possibly even breakfast. I chopped peppers and topped pizzas with them. I sautéed and added them to spaghetti sauces. I tossed them into omelets.

During the summer of tomatoes, I made lots of bacon, lettuce, and tomato sandwiches. I added them to salads. I served them as a side dish. Zucchinis were roasted, steamed, and sautéed as an accompaniment to a meal. They were inserted in stir-fries and spaghetti sauces.

Eating seasonally was a thing I learned in theory years ago but had yet to apply in my daily life. It involved consuming food fresh from the garden or from local farmers, like watermelon in the summer but never in the winter. This approach meant I often ate the same thing repeatedly for several weeks. Whatever I lost in food diversity over short periods, I gained in flavor, freshness, and joy.

Still, there was a problem with all this plenty. When I realized I could not consume my harvest as quickly as it arrived, I looked for ways to preserve my vegetables. I started with freezing.

My research indicated that I could preserve peppers with a simple method. It involved washing them, cutting them up, spreading them on a cookie sheet, laying the sheet in the freezer, allowing individual freezing of pepper pieces, and storing them in a sealed container. This technique preserved the peppers and allowed me to retrieve as few or as many as desired for cooking.

Learning to store the excess of plentiful vegetables and retrieve them in the off-season helped me appreciate my garden even more.

Growing seasons do not last forever. Neither do economic booms and stock market gains or selling seasons for cable TV subscriptions, new mobile phones, and no-doc mortgages.

At the end of cycles, I have witnessed bewilderment, anger, and disillusionment among people who thrived for a season. One day, they harvested overflowing amounts of tomatoes, earned high salaries, and generated more sales commissions than they ever dreamed possible. The next, they plucked vegetables off their vines before tomorrow's expected frost, struggled to make mortgage payments, and wondered why their world had changed abruptly.

Recognizing the seasonal, cyclical aspect of food and money can help manage its presence. Bountiful harvests follow periods of dormancy. Companies and industries expand, plateau, contract, and remake themselves. Opportunities arise, fall away, and emerge again. Paychecks, bonuses, and profit-sharing plans balloon, deflate, and fill again. This news may be alarming yet expected.

Relishing seasonal surplus, sharing with others, and setting aside extra for the future illustrate ways to manage plenty. These practices may take the form of enjoying a vacation, establishing an emergency fund, contributing to a retirement account, paying down debt, setting up a donor-advised fund for charitable giving, or buying assets that support thriving in the future.

Changing seasons ought not to cause confusion, anger, or bitterness. They offer the chance to reflect on the end of one growing season and the eventual start of the next.

38

Celebrate Good Fortune

THE GARDENING CLASS AND my newfound courage to learn hands-on skills encouraged me to plant a vegetable garden, the one in which the amaranth grew tall. This venture marked my second endeavor in gardening that wasn't a complete failure.

Years before, I had arranged for the planting of blueberry bushes. I had asked for a blueberry bush as a Mother's Day gift. My husband bought two, as recommended for pollination.

For whatever reason, only one bush survived. My husband and I remember the reason differently. He says the second bush was planted but died. I remember that the bush was never transplanted from its bucket under the deck into our backyard. Left behind, it withered and died. I felt shame for not planting it myself. Often, when I muster the courage to act, someone offers advice on the proper approach, which contradicts my intended plan. My self-doubt prevents me from even trying.

No matter the circumstances surrounding the planting, just one blueberry bush grew, not two.

A few blueberries had grown over several summers. They were enough to enthuse me but were not bountiful. This remaining bush persisted long enough to apply whatever capabilities I cultivated as a gardener. I plotted how to receive a bigger crop, having either forgotten or dismissed the pollination rule.

Last year, my blueberry bush yielded many bowls of berries, its most bountiful year.

I speculated that my pruning for the first time contributed to the abundance. A gardening book my son gave me for my birthday mentioned pruning to increase my harvest. It seemed crazy that breaking off a few twigs could lead to a banner year for berries.

Due to past experiences in which things died, I hesitated to touch a thriving plant, even one not living up to its potential. I preferred a hands-off approach, not simply out of laziness but a desire to rely on nature with minimal involvement from me. The pruning thing made sense, though. Jesus talks about pruning in the Bible, so I figured it would be a smart move.

I snapped a handful of brittle twigs off a few branches and told myself to return for more extensive and precise pruning later. But I never did that second round.

Minor tweaks and mysteries like these have me marveling at serendipity's role in gardening. Planting, pruning, watering, and weeding improve the opportunity for success. However, uncontrollable variables encourage or impede growth. Certain elements, such as the timing of frosts, the amount of sunshine relative to cloud cover, and the inches of rain that fall in a season, contribute according to a cosmic schedule.

I'll mention again that I have only one blueberry bush. Growing blueberries with only one bush is an anomaly. Generally, cross-pollination requires two plants. As a newbie gardener, I think this term tells me the following: Plant two bushes because that (one) blueberry bush is not going to pollinate itself! Pollination is enigmatic to me, but I hear it's necessary for growth.

Likewise, my saving and investing have borne fruit. Whether my profit reaping was due to my efforts or a mysteriously good run with the stock market is unclear.

Shares of a company's stock I have held for more than thirty years have grown at double the rate of the largest companies in the United States combined, as represented by the S&P 500. The difference in growing wealth over time is significant. (This stock price increased by about 15 percent annually for thirty years, whereas the S&P 500 grew approximately 7.5 percent during the same time. A $10,000 investment returning an annual average of 7.5 percent for thirty years increases to approximately $88,000; at 15 percent, it grows to over $650,000.)

Experts tried to dissuade me from holding so much of one company in favor of more diversified holdings. I resisted the recommendations. Instead, I sold shares periodically for spending, diversification, and giving. Cash generated from these sales funded home improvements, college expenses, travel, a cash reserve, contributions to a Roth 401(k), and shares of handpicked companies. In addition, transfers of shares supported charitable giving, including the start and replenishment of a donor-advised fund.

I may not have heeded all expert advice. But, like planting and nurturing the sole blueberry bush, I was careful. While I clung to shares of a specific company, I also recognized when I needed professional guidance.

For a few years, with another set of accounts, our money did not grow at the pace I expected, despite my careful research into asset allocation and fund selection. Plus, I felt overwhelmed and intimidated by the responsibility of controlling our entire portfolio. My husband and I engaged the services of an outside wealth management firm to manage money amassed within various retirement accounts. In the meantime, I pursued greater knowledge of personal finance and investing.

The spring after the minor winter pruning, I noticed a lot of buds on my blueberry bushes. These turned into actual blueberries. They were small and not yet sweet. This state persisted for longer than I expected.

What might I do better?

I quizzed a friend who I admire as knowledgeable about fruit gardening. She revealed the secret to bringing budding blueberries to ripeness: rain. Rain would plump the blueberries.

Our area needed rain, something I came to appreciate as an adult. Finally, it rained. Then, the blueberries attained perfection.

Drawing on her words of wisdom, I developed the ability to detect rain-induced plumpness in a ripe, sweet berry. Every day or so, for what seemed like weeks, I picked fresh berries to accompany breakfast oatmeal and lunchtime salads as well as serve as a delicious snack.

When I think about my blueberry harvest this year, I count myself lucky. With little attention and an unintentional violation of the cross-pollination rule, I hauled in fresh blueberries.

Just as good fortune plays a role in gardening, luck (a convergence of circumstances not readily predicted and never guaranteed) influences financial success.

While clearing out old files—one of my pandemic projects—I came upon a corporate news release my husband had retained. Its title referenced restructuring. My husband believed this move saved the company, the one with the shares we held for longer than others suggested. The press information discussed the executives' decision to update the design of the retailer's stores. Not only did this move grow sales and profits, but it also positioned the company for significant growth over the long term.

Though implemented by my husband and his colleagues, one decision made by people unknown to me changed the business's destiny—and my own.

Last year's blueberry harvest may be attributable to good fortune, providence, small amounts of work, patience, or a combination of these.

Recently I learned that certain kinds of blueberry bushes are self-fertile, meaning they pollinate themselves.

When I asked for the bush for Mother's Day many years ago, I acted on what I knew at the time: Planting a blueberry bush could lead to a blueberry harvest. Blueberries seemed likely to thrive in my yard better than other fruits such as pineapples or coconuts that require a warmer climate. I nurtured the bush the best I knew. Over time, I was rewarded with a bounty.

My approach and success with investing followed a similar trajectory. Using what I knew, I started, stayed the course, possibly got lucky, and reaped a harvest of growth.

39

Appreciate the Seasons

LAST YEAR IN SEPTEMBER, my blueberry bush stopped bearing blueberries. Buds and berries disappeared. For a time, the leaves remained, letting me know it was still alive. Then the leaves fell away, leaving twiglike remains. The bush in late fall and winter looked different from the one in the summer of plenty.

Often, my investments, particularly stocks, behave like my blueberry bush. They stay dormant for long periods. Then they come to life and overflow with growth. Next, they stop producing for months, sometimes years. Later, they may disappoint me with few berries or thrill me with a bountiful harvest.

A blueberry bush producing fruit year-round sounds terrific. I would welcome small numbers of berries throughout the year instead of a big haul over a short time. Ditto if my investments would rise in price steadily over time instead of falling and rising sharply. This expectation seems reasonable for the shares of companies with consistent sales, stable gross margins, steady cash flow, and low debt. However, even steadily producing businesses fluctuate in price, just as my bush delivers fruit unevenly.

Even before becoming an investor and gardener, I noticed seasonal patterns. Tides came in and out, leaves fell when the days shortened, and flowers bloomed when temperatures warmed. The specifics varied each year, but changes were rhythmic and expected.

By nature, I adore summer, even with its heat and humidity. As a kid, I loved playing with friends at the creek, swimming at a neighborhood pool, and riding my bike during the extended break from school. Even today, the long days of summer energize me. I mourn the change of seasons when the sun casts long shadows and the temperatures cool.

Enjoying fall and winter has required sustained effort for me. To achieve this goal, I forced myself to hike, run, and occasionally cycle in cold weather. I invested in winter gear that includes base layers, wool socks, arm warmers, tights, and specialty gloves. I trained myself to see beauty in bare trees and winter landscapes with the sun low in the sky.

An example of my success in dealing with winter is a standout hike in below-freezing weather that involved more than twenty-five creek crossings. The path took my husband and me from an unmarked, dusty trailhead to an abandoned cabin within the confines of Doughton Park along the Blue Ridge Parkway.

At the start, we tested and verified each rock's stability in the water, avoiding wet shoes, socks, and feet while plodding across the creek beds. As we encountered another crossing, then another, we realized we would not finish the hike by sundown if we continued with this method. We didn't want to get caught outside in the dark, still needing to find our way to the parking lot.

Like my eventual approach to rocky market conditions, we faced a choice: abandon the effort or change our methods. We decided to walk in the creek bottoms and soak our shoes, socks, and feet rather than maneuver each step and risk falling and getting wet anyway. With this change, our progress became swift. Also, I learned the benefits of staying calm in varying conditions and the value of wool socks, which retain heat even while wet.

Even though I prefer summer's greenery, growth, and glow, I accept the coolness and grayness of winter and its precursor, fall. Likewise, though I favor consistent growth in the value of my investments, I accept stillness.

40

Expect Crises

Accepting natural rhythms is one thing. Yet another is learning to deal with catastrophe. What happens when the world changes drastically?

Since the pandemic's start in 2020, the world has changed in ways I never imagined.

Months earlier, I set up alerts in an investing app to aid me in my quest to acquire more shares of Mastercard. At the time, the price seemed high. On the chance the price might fall, I wanted to be alerted to a buying opportunity.

One of the first indications the world was changing was that watch list alerts woke me from a deep sleep, more than once. Why did stock prices keep falling?

The timing was awkward. My husband and I had traveled to New Zealand to celebrate our anniversary. Alerts arrived at odd hours on days different from their sending (we crossed the International Date Line when we flew there). I craved information, but I wanted to enjoy my trip in the relatively carefree days before the virus spread and travel became limited.

In the weeks before we left our home in the United States in early March, a couple of acquaintances predicted the world would be turned upside down by the pandemic. Markets would be affected, they said.

This doomsday message was not the first one I'd ever heard. For several years, experts argued that stock prices had rocketed to astronomical highs and would soon tumble down.

There were a few reasons I held investments even when alarms sounded. Some of my investments sat in regular taxable accounts. I preferred risking temporary value declines to guaranteed cash flow drains to pay taxes.

Further, when market rebounds occurred, gains often came in gushes, not trickles. Even if I could sell at highs, I would need to rebuy at lows before price jumps. Foretelling precise movement was not within my capability.

I often disagreed with experts about unrealistically high valuations. Generally, they referenced the stock market in aggregate, not specific companies. Even when prices rose genuinely higher than warranted, not every company was overpriced and poised for a disastrous fall. I analyzed and tracked the value of the companies I owned, so I had an inkling of whether the share prices of my holdings were too high or not.

My technique for valuing companies is not flawless. Perfection requires foretelling the future and being realistic about economic prospects. I tend to imagine the future as a better version of today, a time when problems are confronted and overcome. In some cases, the companies I own may lead the forefront of solving those problems, such as offering personalized medical treatments or reliable payment processing to support commerce worldwide. Still, my optimism did not mean I could predict sales and revenue growth.

When the virus's presence became a pandemic, I did not know what would happen next. I was familiar with global infectious diseases, such as Ebola, SARS, whooping cough, and polio. However, I had no idea what this novel coronavirus, and COVID-19, the illness it caused, meant on a day-to-day basis or how it might impact the economy and the growth of companies I owned as a shareholder.

Soon, I learned. The uncertainty of the virus's impact, along with the certainty of economic slowdown, led to a massive sell-off and fall in stock prices.

To combat the gloom of this precipitous fall in value, I returned to a time-tested practice for controlling my emotions and behaviors: I did not look. I did not check stock prices. I did not review 401(k) balances or investment account statements.

My decision came from my experience with previous world-altering events, such as the devastation of 9/11 and the global financial crisis affecting the stock, real estate, and jobs markets simultaneously during the Great Recession.

Based on the stream of alerts, I knew things were bad. Mastercard shares kept falling. Using these signals, I intended to buy low. I acquired a few more shares of this company. When the price kept falling, I decided to wait until things settled down.

Serendipitously, by the time I absorbed the severity of the market's reaction, it was too late for me to sell at reasonable prices. Why lock in the results of bad news?

I practiced serenity about my money and my next steps, even as messages from concerned friends and my sister flooded my phone and inbox. They may have believed I was oblivious to the world's happenings. But I was not. Topics of discussion with my traveling companions included the virus, health care rationing, drive-through testing, the stock market, border closings, and stateside toilet paper shortages.

Regarding my readiness, I had a small stash of toilet paper purchased from Costco sitting in my basement. (Disclosure: I own shares of COST.) I also had a case of wine bought from a local vineyard. I felt ready for our eventual return home.

That reminded me of what to do in a crisis (besides staying calm, holding on, and not looking): learn. Not everyone had the luxury to cope with abrupt changes in how the world ran, but I believed I did.

What I absorbed from the past was to ignore ups and downs inconsequential to long-term growth. Sock away cash to buy companies on my watch lists and avoid selling investments at depressed prices to pay bills. Invest in companies I believe will persist in bad times and thrive in good ones. Reduce my dependence on outside resources without divorcing myself from the world.

Becoming more independent was one of the reasons I started my garden.

41

Pursue the Pesky Tasks

My husband and I left New Zealand as the country closed its borders. We arrived back in the United States safely without incident or illness. The value of our investments had been decimated with a major holding down nearly 50 percent (I found out later; as I said, I didn't look) as we awaited better days in the market and the world.

Upon our return, we busied ourselves with work and pandemic-related work-arounds, and I found more pleasure in my garden. However, my budding ability to overcome my weaknesses and do things like growing a garden hadn't transferred to improvements in my visual skills and capability to create beauty in a natural setting.

In the summer of the first year of the pandemic, friends on Facebook displayed photos of their pristine vegetable gardens. Rows of soon-to-be veggies aligned with each other, greenery abounded, and weeds were absent. Martha Stewart's design spirit lived inside their well-tended plots of land and raised garden beds.

Meanwhile, my garden was in disarray. My zucchini plants burst in many directions, with large leafy greens, long yellow flowers, and green speckled vegetables hidden under the foliage. Weeds inhabited half the garden, leaving remnants of what might have been. There were peppers the size of pencil erasers and tomatoes the size of ping-pong balls, never maturing, robbed of nutrients by the unrestrained mess.

In years past, I had blamed my vacations for my failure to weed. One summer was an epic hike in the Alps of France, Italy, and Switzerland. I was gone three weeks in July, plus before and after the trip to settle my younger son in college. Another summer involved a family wedding in the United Kingdom, in which I visited Edinburgh, the Isle of Skye, and London, two weeks away in July and August. One year, I took a weeklong bike trip from Pittsburgh to Washington, DC, along trails converted from railways and canal ways, followed by another week for a mission trip in Kentucky. These activities kept me from my garden and allowed the weeds to gain ground.

Last year, however, I remained home the entire summer. And yet, the weeds persisted. I devoted twenty minutes per day to weeding. This task seemed nearly unbearable, even though spending hours riding my bike outside felt enjoyable. In planning for the next year, I vowed to strengthen my weeding muscles and tolerance for the tedium of pulling weeds.

In my financial life, pesky financial tasks conjure the comparison to weeds. They include reviewing credit card statements for errant charges, unsubscribing to services no longer wanted, keeping records of home improvements, gathering tax information, and following up with people handling aspects of our financial lives. Dealing with these issues is tedious, takes longer than expected, and sometimes fails to make a difference. More to-do items arise after the first batch is completed, so the work is never done.

My husband worked on a weed-like financial task for several months. He requested quotes for our homeowners and auto insurance, hoping for a better deal while maintaining the coverage we wanted.

Our circumstances had changed recently, so revisiting the policies made sense. First, our sons started living on their own, so we did not need to cover them. Second, my husband and his siblings inherited the old family farmland and he needed to add insurance for this property. Lastly, our longtime insurance agent sold his book of business to another agency, prompting us to review prices.

We wanted to retain an odd but desirable clause: earthquake coverage for the house. My husband advised each agency he approached to include all present provisions in its quote.

We live in North Carolina, in a region prone to high winds and heavy rains from hurricanes and the occasional tornado. Soon after we moved into our home, I learned of a fault line affecting the area. Earthquakes existed as a possibility, even though they had not happened before, as far as I knew. Why not add a rider to protect the house, not our largest asset, but a sizable one?

Several years ago, after adding the earthquake provision, I sat in my sunroom and felt shaking. Previously, I had experienced earthquakes through books, movies, newspaper accounts, and television shows only. Intuitively, though, I knew the shaking resulted from an earthquake.

I checked a definitive source to confirm. It was Facebook certified; others had felt it also.

Soon after, I received a postcard from my insurance guy. It read: "You don't have earthquake insurance. You can get earthquake insurance from us."

I called my insurance agent. I asked him why I received this notice because I *did* have earthquake insurance, a rider on my homeowners insurance, something I had arranged years before.

Checking his records, my insurance agent confirmed coverage. He explained that the national network sent a postcard blast to drum up business, not something he endorsed, but it was helpful in communicating coverage availability.

"Okay, I just wanted to make sure," I said while wondering why the company's system did not cross-reference its mailing with customers who maintained the earthquake rider.

Several years elapsed with no perceptible shaking from earthquakes, but I kept the coverage, or so I thought. Then 2020 appeared, labeled as the year of weird stuff happening, even when these things have happened before.

One morning, I felt movement. We live along the flight pattern of medical helicopters rushing victims to a trauma hospital. Sometimes when they fly over, the flutter of helicopter rotors reverberating, the house seems to shake. When a hurricane or cold front comes through, I can hear the wind's effects on the trees outside and feel something similar.

I listened for helicopters and trees swaying due to wind. There were none. The movement was noticeable and persistent. My husband, also in the house at the time, asked if I was moving something, perhaps causing this unusual noise stemming from the shaking.

"No, dear," I told him. "We're having an earthquake."

Again, Facebook came through for me. Others felt it too. Later, the news reports confirmed an earthquake in Sparta, a small mountain town seventy miles away.

I did not worry about our investment in the house. We had earthquake insurance. No more ruminating about this topic was required. I returned to whatever I had been doing.

My husband had an uneasy feeling. After getting quotes from a few companies, he had stuck with our original provider because it was the only agency that would cover the farm. He had insisted it maintain all elements of our previous policies, absent our children's coverage. However, when he checked the documents after this second incident, he could not find the reference to the earthquake rider. We did have it before, as I'd confirmed with policy papers stored at the house. The rider had been dropped in the most recent policy renewal.

Verifying the earthquake coverage reminded me of weeding, an annoying task that makes things better but could be escaped if life worked how we wanted. My husband could have avoided follow-up if the insurance agency's employees had heeded his instructions. Instead, he found himself dealing with this unpleasant task, a small thing that could become a big problem.

He left phone messages and sent emails to the agency. After several days, he received a response. The insurance company had omitted the rider.

After being prompted, the agent added, "So sorry for the inconvenience."

I had become accustomed to our longtime agent, who took care of stuff for us. Sadly, there are times the person who is supposed to handle something does not. Checking behind others is another weeding task. It's tedious but necessary.

We have earthquake coverage now. I am still working on attaining the perfect garden.

42

Do What You Can

GARDENING AND ITS COUSIN, yardwork, calm me. These hobbies provide opportunities to notice nature and shape my surroundings.

Still, I wrestle with allocating my time to upkeep and improvement. During the winter, there is little to do. During the summer, there can be loads to accomplish, such as harvesting my garden's production and pulling weeds. The timing can be awkward, as it is often brutally hot outside during the day. Often, I join friends for bike rides in the early mornings and late afternoons, the best times for gardening.

I have experimented with several upkeep methods, allotting a certain number of minutes daily or designating an entire day for outside care. These approaches have improved my productivity and sense of peace about what I accomplish and what's left undone.

Yet, I fear the work will never be done. I could always mess around outside, finding a patch of land that needed grass seed, a weed to be pulled, a tree to be trimmed, or a fallen limb to be moved to the yard waste area. On the other hand, I do not want to spend inordinate amounts of time trying to create perfection, especially when my notion of excellence keeps evolving.

When I consider never-ending garden tasks, I realize that long lists of must-dos may affect my finances in a similar way. Some effort improves results but also points to more activity. Where does this tidying up, trimming back, and researching the best technique end?

43

Run from Senseless Activity

As a money manager, you may fear endless efforts with no payoff. Before becoming a gardener, I feared never-ending work and a lack of results.

When my kids were younger, several years before I started my garden, I read and reread *Bear and Bunny Grow Tomatoes* by Bruce Koscielniak to them. This book captured my feelings about gardening.

In the book, Bear toiled at removing rocks from his gardening plot. He hunted for rocks to remove so he could create the perfect spot for growing tomatoes. His relentlessness in preparing the soil before planting made me tired.

Bunny, meanwhile, did nothing to prepare. When the time came for planting, he threw seeds in the yard and hoped for the best.

Bear and Bunny were opposites. Bear was über-diligent. He followed all the rules and grew a magnificent garden of tomatoes. Bunny tried a hit-and-miss approach. His garden yielded nothing. In the end, Bear shares his harvest with Bunny.

You might be concerned that the book celebrates laziness. After all, Bunny received tomatoes without putting in the work done by Bear. Yes, Bunny received tomatoes despite his lack of effort. But I identified with Bunny, not because I look for tomato handouts but because Bear's gardening protocol appeared over-the-top.

Sometimes, experts—in both the financial and gardening worlds—seem to recommend extra work for no reason except to suggest activity is preferable to inactivity, complexity to simplicity.

As a beginning gardener, you may feel doomed to failure if you do not locate and remove all rocks from the soil, nurture seedlings before transferring to an outdoor garden, spray fruit trees to prevent bug infestations, and routinely test and treat the soil.

As a novice money manager, you may feel pressured to track every expense, hurry up and start investing (but only in what you understand completely), figure out whether your tax bracket in retirement will be higher or lower than your current one (to determine whether to fund a Roth or traditional account), save all your medical receipts in your thirties so you can extract money tax-free from your HSA in your seventies, and periodically refinance your mortgage to reduce your payment or obtain a better rate.

These may be helpful tactics to grow your garden and grow your wealth. But pursuing all possible advantages may be paralyzing, which will not move you forward.

As a blossoming gardener, I wanted to focus on the essentials and ignore the rest. Not only would this approach help me begin, but it would also allow me to succeed as I returned to these foundations again and again.

Doing things merely to do them, particularly in gardening, repelled me. Similarly, specific money tasks attractive to me—such as scrutinizing differences among health insurance plans or analyzing the cash flow of potential investments—may be tedious and even unnecessary to others. Focusing on peripheral items can detract from pursuing financial freedom.

44

Notice Details

FOR PEOPLE LIKE ME who love finances and accompanying analysis, however, peripheral items are often where the fun lies.

"Would it be better to a) pay off high-interest debt or b) invest in my employer's 401(k) that offers an automatic match?" you ask.

"Oh, let me design a spreadsheet and give you a proper answer," I respond with heartfelt happiness.

When I prepare my soil for planting seeds, usually by breaking it up with a metal garden instrument, I often hear *clink*.

This distinct sound tells me I have struck a hardened thing. I am amazed at the number of rocks in the dirt! Year after year, I hear *clink, clink, clink*. Every time I hear that noise and then find and remove a rock, I think of Bear, the character in the children's book.

Have I become Bear?

I do not want to be Bear!

I am NOT Bear!

Here is the difference between Bear and me: Bear seems to seek out the rocks, whereas I discover them along the way.

Every discipline has rocks: quirky things experts unearth and then emphasize at the wrong time, making competency for nonexperts more complicated than necessary. Money rocks may include taxes, credit scores, insurance deductibles, detailed budgets, and the debt vs investing question.

What I realize, though, is I may seem like the Bear of money when I write about financial intricacies, such as the tax consequences of holding mutual funds compared to individual stocks. In my defense, I do not seek out this knowledge. It comes to me with experience, the way my time in the garden leads me to clink against rocks.

Likewise, I do not hunt for financial dilemmas and fine print but deal with them when they surface. My intention is to ignore the rocks and focus on the essentials.

45

Experiment

As I mentioned earlier, my instruction and burgeoning knowledge of gardening spread to other areas of my life, namely my yard. I bought grass seed from a source recommended by a friend.

On a warm fall day, my husband threw some of this grass seed on bare patches left by a recently removed chain link fence. Almost overnight, the seeds sprouted and grew. Bright green grass stood out in my backyard, a beacon of unexpected success.

The seed company's instructions specified waiting to sow grass until after the first few touches of frost. Such timing allowed the seeds to lie dormant during the winter and then awaken to life in the spring.

Without consulting me or the instructions, my husband planted those seeds right before heavy rains swept through the area.

There was a risk the grass would not persist through the winter. Early sowing could end in ruin, despite the initial success. On the other hand, spreading the seed was worth a try. The dirt patches would have turned into a muddy mess from the torrential rains expected from a string of hurricanes.

The timing seemed convenient. Science and math, however, do not always bend to my convenience. My hopefulness alone does not sustain a field of grass during the winter, deliver a batch of tomatoes in the summer, or give me an investment portfolio to support me while I'm not working a full-time job.

So, about those instructions built on scientific research: Are they immovable or mere suggestions? Are they meant to guide, not dictate?

What I discovered about instructions printed on seed packets and bags: They are concise and valuable. They do not, however, relate the entire body of knowledge for gardening and lawn care. Instead, they offer guidelines to deliver success to most time-squeezed, limited-attention-span, make-it-easy-for-me home gardeners.

Experiments, including those deviating from official rule books, advance my knowledge of how things work. Whether seeds or cash, they are ideal for extras but should not form the core strategy for gardening or growing wealth.

46

Do Nothing

I MENTIONED I MEANT to prune my blueberries over the winter last year, beyond snapping a few twigs. Failing to act resulted partly from hesitation and partly from forgetfulness.

A gardening friend advised me to prune sparingly. I decided not to overdo my intervention, then forgot about the task during the dark winter months.

Being too aggressive with actions like pruning can harm growing things, just as too much water may have killed my cactus years ago. The bush delivered a bountiful harvest last year, with minimal effort on my part.

Knowing when to act and when to do nothing to produce specific results is not always easy. I tend to do as little as possible when I'm unsure of the benefits of my actions.

When growing wealth, like blueberries, doing less may yield better results than doing more.

A few people asked me what they should do after share prices plunged at the start of the pandemic. One couple mentioned that their financial advisor recommended inaction, and my friends questioned the soundness of this advice.

I have qualms about contradicting professionals, especially those who know or should know the specifics of their clients' needs. In this case, though, there was little hesitation on my part as I concurred with the professional advice. Doing nothing seemed a reasonable course of action.

I perceived the presence of three fundamental choices: Do nothing and hope prices returned to normal soon. Sell shares before prices fall further. Buy shares at bargain prices before they rebound. I felt unsure what would happen next, whether prices would continue falling or rise back to what I perceived as normal. Do nothing surfaced as the easiest choice, requiring no follow-up activities.

This course of inaction yielded good results for me. (The holding that lost half its value rebounded and grew fourfold from its low by the end of 2020.)

My point, though, is not that I was wise or lucky, or that my resolve paid off. Things could have easily turned out differently. My argument is that doing nothing can be a legitimate choice. There are appropriate times to prune, water, or add nutrients to the soil, just as there are times to do nothing to allow my garden to thrive.

The Connections Takeaway

Find the types of gardening and wealth growing you enjoy and pursue them to thrive physically, financially, and emotionally. Growth is often seasonal, so learn to set aside surplus, alternate diligence with rest, and appreciate bounty. There are foundational principles to growing a garden and wealth but no guarantees.

The Groundwork: Get Your Tools

47

Understand Growth

To START A GARDEN, I needed direct, explicit, and detailed instruction. I craved clarity on the essentials, so I could ignore the endless recommendations for things like seed incubators, crop rotations, sprays for pests, and irrigation. I wanted a small success upon which to build my understanding.

Growing wealth, or at least getting started in this endeavor, seemed more straightforward. The messages came clearly in my language: numbers and literal interpretation of words.

My education in money started early. A momentous lesson from elementary school came from a teacher's illustration of compound interest. It originated with the teacher asking my classmates and me whether we would rather receive a penny each day, doubled over the previous day for an entire month, or a dollar each day for a month, consisting of thirty-one days.

Even with above-average math skills, I struggled to imagine a cent could grow much in a month. At first glance, the dollar a day sounded better than the penny, giving us $31—a large sum in those days.

However, when my classmates and I did the math, we were astounded to discover a penny doubled every day gave us over $10 million in one month.

This lesson taught me exponential growth, a valuable concept for understanding compounding. Applying this principle proved tricky, though, as I could not find a bank paying 100 percent interest daily.

For practical insight about compounding growth, I learned from my parents.

One Saturday, a few years after my teacher's illustration, my dad held his mortgage passbook open at the kitchen table. Passbooks were issued in the days before digital dashboards. They enabled bank customers to keep their personal records of account balances associated with savings accumulations and loan payoffs. These books were updated with each transaction, allowing you to verify the accuracy of the bank's records compared to yours.

Dad's mortgage passbook was a small book with lined pages containing scribbles and stamps proclaiming mortgage balances, interest charges, and payments applied to principal and interest, distributed more heavily to principal and less to interest over time. Using it as a guide, my dad explained the mechanics of mortgages.

This kitchen table lesson helped me understand the idea of compounding growth concretely. I could see what was happening to my parents' money, expressed in dollars and cents on the family's home loan. Given this glimpse into personal finance, I quickly understood debt payoff and its reverse, wealth building.

Just as I envisioned possibilities from a passbook, a gardener may visualize the potential in a seed. Cultivated, this tiny object may blossom into vegetables, grains, nuts, herbs, or fruit, containing seeds for the future. These small beginnings may be extracted and sown, multiplying the yield of the original seed. Exponential growth is not only a math concept but also a natural one.

Considering the daily doubling of a penny and the payoff of a mortgage, I understood from a young age that everyday decisions carry financial consequences—these consequences compound, either for or against me.

48

Learn the Latest Rules

More lessons arrived at home.

The house where my dad lived as a child—his parents' home—was repossessed when he was young. So was a bike he received for Christmas. It was the early 1930s, the time of the Great Depression.

He told me these stories often—not with bitterness but with the recollection of what this historic time felt like for a young child.

My dad explained that mortgages in the Depression tended to be short-term loans, say five years, not the fifteen or thirty years more common today. At the end of the term, borrowers owed the entire balance, like the balloon payments of today. Typically, homeowners would take out another mortgage loan to pay off this balance. However, when credit tightened before and during the Depression, borrowers could not obtain new mortgages. As a result, many lost their homes. These scenarios repeated themselves, resulting in foreclosures like those experienced by my grandparents.

The housing market was so bad and money so scarce no one else could afford to buy the house where my grandparents, uncle, and dad lived. So, they stayed put. My understanding is that the lender took ownership of the house, replaced the roof and made other improvements to position it for resale, and then resold the home back to my grandparents—with a new, manageable mortgage.

Federal housing legislation and actions taken by lenders reversed the downward spiral of the housing industry and made mortgage borrowing friendlier to consumers, at least for some of them.

The ability to purchase a home and then control and eventually eliminate fixed expenses is a key to financial stability for many people. Further, a predictable economy with opportunities to earn income, invest, and protect assets supports the pursuit of financial freedom.

Likewise, the presence or availability of good soil, water, and sunshine and the absence of difficult weather-related events, such as droughts, floods, and damaging storms, support a flourishing garden.

Even though circumstances for thriving may not be ideal at certain times, knowing how financial systems work can empower me to make smarter decisions.

49

Discover Why Time Matters

Years after learning about compound growth, one of the most critical lessons from college centered on the *time value of money*. I studied business and finance at UNC, and this concept became a singular force in managing my finances.

The time value of money signifies how money today differs in value from money yesterday and money tomorrow. For example, in an economy with excellent investment opportunities, a dollar today is worth more than a dollar tomorrow and less than the day before.

Likewise, the value of a seed today differs from the worth of its harvest tomorrow. If you sow a seed properly and the conditions for thriving are present, the seed's value is more than its tiny presence today. Its value can be represented by its worth derived from the vegetables, fruit, and grains you harvest in the future.

To compare present and future values, both representing the time value of money, let's return to the imaginary world my elementary school teacher described where I could earn 100 percent interest for thirty-one days. To make a fair comparison, I consider either the current value of each choice at the beginning of the month (present value) or their values at the end of the month, on the thirty-first day (future value).

I'll increase the value of the cash payout at the end of the month from $31 to $500,000. So, there are two choices: today's value of one cent or the end-of-the-month value of a half-million dollars. To make apples-to-apples comparisons, I compare the two present values and the two future values. The future value of $0.01 equals $10,737,418, which is greater than the other choice of $500,000. Put another way, the present values of the two offers equal $0.01 (the penny) and $0.00046566 (the $500,000 promise at the end of the month). Given a choice between a) one cent ($0.01) today or b) a half-million dollars ($500,000) on the last day of the month, I would choose the penny today.

The magnitude and certainty of investment growth vary in the real world, but the concept endures.

50

Go with the Flows

A NUMBERS AND MONEY person like me revels in the time-value notion. Soon after learning about time values, I realized that financial products, services, and decisions could be expressed as a series of cash flows. Time value is conceptual, whereas cash flow is the practical application of this concept.

Whether you are choosing between a penny today or a half-million dollars in thirty-one days, an annual payout or lump sum for lottery winnings, a job offer with a pension or one promising equity in the company (rarely both!), investing within a traditional or Roth retirement account, or a million other things, financial decisions can be considered in terms of time value and distilled to cash flow.

Examples abound. Working for an employer generates a series of regular paychecks and perhaps a year-end bonus, providing cash flowing into your bank account. A home mortgage involves a series of payments flowing out of your bank account, starting with a down payment and continuing with monthly payments until you pay the loan in full. An annuity requires cash from the customer in exchange for a promise from the insurance company to deliver payments in the future.

An insurance policy involves cash flowing from the customer (the insured) to the insurance company (the insurer) through regular payment of premiums. Later, when the insured files a claim covered by the insurer and receives reimbursement, money flows from the company to the customer. There are also possible costs, such as co-pays and caps on out-of-pocket expenses, which can be expressed as cash flows.

Here's an example with dollars attached.

Let's say you land a job that offers a 401(k) account with a 3 percent match. You decide to contribute $5,000 to the 401(k), qualifying you for the match. In the first year of your participation in the retirement plan, your holdings grow in value by 7 percent. The contribution lowers your income for tax purposes by $1,100 (using a 22 percent tax rate). At the end of the year, your account balance equals $5,500.

Your initial outlay is $5,000, the inflow associated with the tax reduction is $1,100, and your net cash outlay is $3,900. Inside the retirement account, you receive $150 as a company match and $350 in added value through the investment growth; I won't count those as cash flows (outlays) because that money didn't come from your paycheck or bank account.

In this scenario, the contribution of $5,000 and company match of $150 are guaranteed (that is, if you add $5K to your retirement account, that amount will be deposited, and according to the plan guidelines, you'll receive the matching amount). The tax benefit is variable, depending on your income and tax legislation. The investment gains reflect reality for this particular year. However, investment growth is not guaranteed. When modeling cash flows, I consider what's a sure thing (the money coming out of the paycheck) and what's not (investment growth). Overall, you've set aside $3,900 and now have $5,500, a 40 percent gain.

Let's say you contributed to your workplace retirement account, $5,000 yearly, for twenty years, and you continue to earn the match and get those investment returns. The projected future value of this account is over $200,000. Plus, you'd have received the benefit of lower taxes. The benefit of fewer taxes means more cash available for other uses.

Complexities to this cash flow model could include tax credits for which you become eligible with a lower income, achieved by contributing to a qualified retirement account. These may seem like windfalls available to those with moderate or lower incomes only, but even those with relatively high incomes may reap credits, say for children's college expenses.

You'd also want to consider and model cash flow associated with the tax savings generated by the retirement account contributions; these could include paying off credit card debt, taking a trip, saving for a down payment on a house, or investing in a regular brokerage account. Further, there are intangibles that a model can't reproduce, such as the feeling of freedom from paying off debt or the joy of traveling with friends.

When you remove the money from the retirement account, you'll owe ordinary income taxes and possibly a penalty if you generate cash before retirement age, as specified by tax rules. The actual money that flows into your life from the 401(k) will equal the withdrawal, less income taxes (and penalties if those apply).

Capturing these series of cash flows and their timelines helps me make financial decisions as well as gauge the worthiness of a financial product or service compared to alternatives. My analysis involves projecting every cash flow item, whether an expense or income, an outlay of cash or receipt of money. I consider whether this flow is guaranteed or hypothetical (also called "illustrative").

Delineating between the two—guaranteed and not guaranteed—is the first step in making my decision. The second is weighing possibilities with likelihoods and acknowledging my emotional bent toward one or the other. Then, I identify what makes sense to me.

As I moved from college to the real world, I carried this idea of the time value of money and applied it to my financial decisions using cash flow models. I envisioned money coming to or going away from me in these scenarios.

Sometimes, I did these calculations in my head as I weighed whether a new dress was worth forgoing shares of a mutual fund I fancied. Later, as digital spreadsheets became commonplace, I used them to measure the costs and benefits of financial moves, such as buying a house with a mortgage, choosing a health plan, and determining whether to fund a traditional or Roth account.

51

Invest for Real

LESSONS FROM INSIDE THE college classroom proved crucial. What I learned outside became as valuable.

During my junior and senior years in college, I worked as a resident advisor for the UNC housing department, where I received real-life insights. One of the full-time department administrators, the woman who had invested in the grocery store chain, was rumored to be rich.

"How exactly does one become independently wealthy?" two of my coworkers asked after pulling me aside for a private conversation inspired by this woman's status.

Today the questions may be "How do I retire early?" "How do I become financially independent?" or "How do I become financially free?"

Their query surprised me, but not because I doubted their desire to become independent and wealthy. What caught me off guard was their lack of understanding of financial markets. They excelled academically and held well-defined career ambitions. They dealt with delicate situations with savvy and grace, grasping and navigating life's challenges with sophistication and wisdom. Until our talk, though, they seemed to know little about investing.

Like me, they had heard that this administrator was independently wealthy. A coworker said she was an original investor in a North Carolina-based grocery store. This investment became the source of her wealth. How this arrangement came to pass prompted the question.

Drawing on talk about the company and my knowledge of investing from finance courses, my understanding of her investment followed a simple storyline. A businessman decided to start and grow a grocery store chain. He asked friends and acquaintances in his hometown for $1,000 each in exchange for an ownership share of the company. About a hundred people came through for him in this word-of-mouth offering—all without national media coverage or investment bankers. The chain expanded, the company's worth grew, and the original investors became rich.

Considering the look on my friends' faces as they absorbed my explanation, I believe I offered insights that helped them understand how and why to start investing.

Likewise, learning garden essentials from an expert started me on the right path. Next, hands-on lessons from my garden reinforced what I learned in the classroom. Noticing what worked for me and what did not work well prompted me to learn more through research and casual conversations about growing things.

As I became more proficient in gardening, I developed the confidence to converse about growing techniques and compare notes with other gardeners.

Occasionally, talk with friends included discussions about rainfall, fruit ripening, early and late frosts, and weed recognition.

The subject of costs vs benefits in gardening and similar pursuits came up at a social gathering. A friend told me she found the effort of tending a vegetable garden to be more taxing than growing fruit from trees. As a result, she decided to focus on cultivating fruit orchards. My observations matched hers, and I, too, decided to plant fruit trees in my backyard to achieve a higher return on my time and money investments.

My investing education took root during my years in college. Investments, like stocks, mutual funds, and ETFs (exchange-traded funds), were not discussed much at home. When I was growing up, stocks carried high costs to buy and sell, and generally, one needed an expensive full-service broker to handle transactions. Mutual funds seemed to be emerging as a popular investment vehicle for middle-class families, possibly due to the introduction of tax-advantaged accounts such as IRAs (individual retirement arrangements). Index funds were still young. ETFs had not yet been invented.

My job and my studies helped me fit the puzzle pieces together. I came to understand how a housing administrator from a small town in North Carolina could make heaps of money independent of a job. I also noticed that she continued to work and draw a salary, fortifying her financial position.

Until my friends asked about growing wealth, investing had seemed abstract. Financial charting, P/E (price/earnings) ratios, and earnings guidance confused me. As I explained and integrated the idea of financial independence, investing crystallized in my mind as something real people do in real businesses. It meant buying a part of a business and trusting its leaders to run the company for good and profit.

This exchange, in which my friends hung on every word, imparted confidence and fueled my desire to invest. Further, their nods of understanding conveyed they now considered stock investing accessible to them as a method of growing wealth.

52

Recognize Conflicts of Interest

A FEW YEARS AFTER college graduation, I began investing as soon as I made room in my budget. During this time, the early 1980s, interest rates soared to historic highs, and the savings and loan crisis loomed.

On a visit to my parents' house, I found my dad again with the mortgage passbook at the kitchen table. I asked him why he did not pay off the mortgage in full. The balance was low, and eliminating this debt looked attractive to me.

He said, "The bank would love for me to do that."

He told me the bank sent him letter after letter requesting a payoff. Similar requests went to others in his situation, those paying low rates of interest on their mortgages. The combined actions of mortgage borrowers settling debts could solve the problems of savings and loans and other financial institutions.

Banks and savings and loans had lent money at low rates, say 4 percent, for thirty years through fixed-rate mortgages in the 1960s. Decades later, they paid 10 percent and more to depositors for cash held in savings accounts. They hoped to eliminate these mortgages sooner rather than later, averting the emerging catastrophe caused by spending more than they earned.

One of my dad's lessons became clear: It did not make sense to apply extra cash to hasten a loan payoff when a government-insured bank account paid more. If I could generate 13 percent in a savings account, there would be no reason to pay off a debt costing 4 percent, except for personal preferences or tax reasons. The financially beneficial choice pointed to earning more interest instead of paying more on debt.

Later in life, I developed an aversion to debt. Eliminating or avoiding debt could form a component of a sound strategy for managing money. For some people, being debt-free brings peace of mind, even if financially, the numbers favor low-interest debt as the better path to growing wealth.

The lesson from this conversation with my dad, however, proved to be more than the math or the feeling of financial freedom. What I learned: A conflict of interest existed between the bank and my dad. The bank urged borrowers to pay off their low-interest loans, with no incentive, rather than earn higher returns in a savings account. Financial institutions did not put their customers' needs above their own, not in this situation and probably not in many others.

I resolved to protect myself from financial institutions. Starting then, I entered these relationships with skepticism instead of trust.

I mentioned earlier that I preferred to plant seeds, not seedlings. Upon reflection, I realize my rationale for this choice is more than the simplicity of this method. It's also been easier for me to find trustworthy seed companies from which to buy seeds than to evaluate the quality and sturdiness of seedlings.

53

Cultivate Instincts

THIS SECOND CONVERSATION WITH my dad about mortgages had happened soon after I graduated from college and entered the workforce. My entry felt rocky, due partly to an economic recession and double-digit unemployment rates.

The decade of my graduation from college was also marked by a flurry of corporate acquisitions orchestrated through LBOs (leveraged buyouts) in which private equity firms borrowed to buy businesses. Acquirers then paid down debt with cash flow from operations or sales of corporate assets.

By my mid-twenties, I had held accounting and finance positions with a regional bank acquired by a larger one and an apparel manufacturer rumored to be ripe for acquisition. I was working for a food company when my employer became a target for a takeover.

Corporate executives held an off-site session to assure us of our job security and the company's brand integrity following an announcement that a competitor was acquiring our employer.

“You know you need to worry about your job when they tell you, ‘Don’t worry about your job,’” my boss said after the meeting as my coworkers and I walked to our cars.

Until that moment, I had believed my boss never held a firm opinion. I would receive direction on a matter in a meeting, only to discover his position reversed in a subsequent one.

I speculated that my boss’s honesty emerged when he realized he no longer needed to engage in corporate politics. After further reflection, I gathered he might have been as frustrated with our work environment as I was. The expediency demanded by higher-ups seemed to eclipse the truth. Whatever the motivation, his casual comment was a rare moment, one I treasured for its humor and clarity.

For much of my life, I labored to decode words. Discerning the true meaning of communications meant deciding whether another person was being straightforward and meticulous about word choice, was attempting to deceive with vague terms, or simply lacked the vocabulary (or thought I did) required to convey ideas with precision.

Interpreting words literally was a hallmark of my cognitive style, which seemed normal to me. It seemed odd that expecting others to mean what they say and say what they mean was considered deviant. Given the arguments due to my confusion and the frequency I was called difficult, however, I conceded my ways of thinking and questioning were atypical.

Being confused by other people's words, sadly, was common for me—whether from an executive promising me my job was secure or a financial professional telling me my money was safe. *Do I trust their words or my discomfort with their claims?*

Over time, I developed coping mechanisms. As people spoke, the equivalent of a calculator appeared in my head. It assigned debits and credits, gains and losses, and assets and liabilities to their statements. For example, a friend may tell me he's doing great when discussing personal finances. Later in the conversation, I may notice his mention of an unexpected car repair bill without a corresponding amount in a savings account. My mental machine recognized when stories did not add up.

To make sense of the world, I also pursued and gathered knowledge, which accumulated and compounded, particularly in business and finance. Numbers and facts did not reveal everything I needed to know, but they gave me insights.

At the time of the company's off-site meeting, I knew my state followed employment-at-will laws, meaning an employer or employee could end the workplace arrangement at any time for any reason except illegal ones. Absent a contract between a company and an employee, no job was guaranteed.

My boss headed the corporate accounting function. He and I knew the acquiring business did not need two accounting departments.

Ultimately, our jobs disappeared. Eventually, the executives also reversed reassurances about preserving the company's brand.

54

Decode Conversations

Eventually, my ability to convert speech to math equations morphed from a habit to a superpower. I didn't equate spending on homes, cars, and vacations with wealth. No, I latched on to remarks about braces for the kids and learned about benefit packages; listened to a concern about payroll taxes and identified cash flow problems within a struggling business; rejoiced in a friend's recovery from a severe medical condition and anticipated hardship from the onslaught of bills; and talked about upcoming trips and uncovered a plan for early retirement.

The stints in corporate accounting and finance had honed my expertise in decoding conversations. I learned to crunch the numbers rather than accept what corporate executives, bankers, and financial sales representatives told me.

I haven't yet developed expertise in gardening. But when I stumble upon a friend's social media post, conversation, or article about plants, I often learn something new. Before learning the essentials and producing vegetables, this talk seemed like a secret language. Now I can make sense of the information, determine where it fits within the essentials' structure, and possibly apply it to my growing situation.

Applying a math-based decision framework helps me evaluate financial services, such as bank accounts, insurance products, and credit card offers. The designs of these vary, so I consider their costs and benefits to determine which ones provide the most value. As I mentioned earlier, my process involves determining the amount and timing of cash outflows as well as cash inflows and other benefits.

For example, I analyze whether a monthly fee on a checking account might offset the waiving of ATM fees and high-interest rates paid on account balances. I consider whether refinancing a mortgage to lower monthly payments makes sense based on closing costs and the loan term's restart, pushing the mortgage payoff date further into the future. I weigh whether the benefit of waived baggage fees counters a travel credit card's annual fee. I compare a lump-sum payout of a pension benefit with a monthly paycheck for life.

Numbers also guide my investing decisions.

As I mentioned earlier, I adopted and refined a system to evaluate individual stocks, drawing on learnings from investment books and my observations of business operations. My approach involves calculating current values based on cash flow projections. I also review financial statements for basics, such as profitability and the availability of cash to pay bills.

I can't predict the cost and benefit of all financial products. Variables like the number of months I might live and collect an annuity paycheck, the frequency with which I may fly and receive free checked bags using my rewards credit card, or how much a company will grow cannot be pinpointed with complete accuracy. But doing the math offers a way to make sound financial decisions, rather than trusting a convincing salesperson, following conventional wisdom, or relying on gut feelings.

Math and spreadsheets became my friends. Rather than taking my cues from social signaling, I translate abstract ideas into figures and formulas. Instead of relying on hope or instinct, I fire up a spreadsheet and do the math.

The Groundwork Takeaway

LEARN HOW COMPOUNDING GROWTH works and how time can work to your advantage. Develop a way to evaluate financial products and services independently. Recognize and accept your biases in making financial decisions.

The Unexpected Development: Grow Beyond the Garden

55

Ignore the Critics

My foray into gardening sparked insights into other areas of my life. Oddly, my yard and garden helped me recognize how public policy and financial inventions informed my choices and affected wealth accumulation. The path to these realizations was winding.

Before the garden, there were a series of yards—places for me to tame, or so I thought. My ground cover attempt had failed, but surely, I could tend a traditional lawn, right?

To contribute to lawn care and surprise my husband, one day while he was away I took out the riding lawnmower and cut the grass. We had recently returned to North Carolina after an out-of-state move and were living in a rental home while we shopped for houses. The rental property needed work, but the backyard was expansive and flat, though marshy in a tiny section.

The riding mower reminded me of what we called a straight drive car, one with a manual transmission, requiring knowledge of using a clutch and a stick shift, which I had mastered out of necessity years before. When I left for college, my parents had two cars in the driveway, one automatic and one manual; I returned the following summer to find two straight drive cars there. To get around town, I needed to learn to drive these cars or walk, ride my bike, or take the bus wherever I wanted to travel. Though the latter options were suitable in many cases, I also wanted to drive in certain situations. My dad taught me, and I added this life skill to my roster of things I could do. Though it was a short list, I was proud of this accomplishment.

The first car I bought and paid for myself boasted a manual transmission. So, I felt confident with the lawnmower, even though it didn't have safety belts or protection between me and the ground.

I had no problem with the grass. The terrain was flat, except for the small marshy area, which I avoided. The cutting proceeded smoothly. I can't recall finesse associated with my technique, but basically, I drove the mower over the lawn in straight lines; if I noticed that I missed a spot, I returned to that section and took care of any stray grass stands. When I finished, the lawn was trimmed.

When my husband saw my handiwork, he told me I had cut the grass wrong. According to him, the proper method required mowing the grass in a circular pattern, not straight rows.

I had never noticed patterns in freshly cut grass and didn't think I ever would. I vowed never to mow the grass again.

You may have made a financial move that pleased you, only to be told you've done the wrong thing or done the right thing but poorly.

You may have decided to eliminate your debt and paid off your smallest loan, only to be told you should have tackled credit card debt because it carries the highest interest rate. You may have bought shares of a thriving company and then read that no one except billionaire investor Warren Buffett is smart enough to choose an individual stock and you should have bought shares of an index fund instead. You may have chosen a high-deductible health plan and then been told that a better choice would have been a plan with co-pays and lower deductibles.

Don't throw up your hands and avoid financial decisions the way I avoided cutting the grass for the next thirty years (and counting). No, celebrate your victories: the paid-off debt, the start of investing, and the selection of a health plan. These will enable you to spend less than you earn, make money without working daily, and protect yourself.

If you'd like, learn more ways to save, invest, and protect; then, sync your moves with your personal preferences and unique situation. For example, if you're more motivated to invest in a company you love, follow that path; if you find comfort in investing in the entire market, focus on index funds. Alternatively, consult a genuine financial professional (not anyone who denigrates or dismisses your initiative) for guidance and insights.

Just as there's no single technique for cutting the grass, there's not just one way to deal with finances.

56

Question Convention

I ABANDONED YARD UPKEEP early in my life as a homeowner. After failing to grow ground cover, hearing I mowed the lawn in an aesthetically displeasing way, and struggling to keep grass green and flowering plants alive, I realized I was stuck in a learning-curve abyss. Rather than claw my way out, I quit.

Freed from lawn care, I busied myself raising children, working, and managing family finances.

One of my reasons for not caring about my lawn's persistent imperfection is that relatively few noticed its curbside appearance due to its location, tucked deep into the neighborhood. Further, for many years, the grounds on one side bordered the backyards of a series of lawn-indifferent owners, including a bank that had foreclosed on my neighbor's property.

Beauty is in the eye of the beholder, I reasoned. My husband, teenage neighbors, and my sons cut grass and weeds. I arranged for trees in peril of falling to be taken down. That was all. My desire to learn gardening remained a twinkle in my eye.

Then, new neighbors arrived following the foreclosure. They cleaned their yard and their home's exterior.

With their arrival, which coincided with our empty nest, my husband and I decided to become more diligent in exterior care. He hired a landscaper to deal with longstanding weedy areas and redo the front yard with rolled sod, which produced an instantly manicured lawn.

A natural area next to the house became a vegetable garden.

When I started my garden, I chose a section of land that received full sun, a gardening essential for the tomatoes and other vegetables I wanted to grow. It happened to be in my side yard, next to the house and in full view from the street. I didn't consider how the garden's aesthetics might affect my home's curb appeal.

Restrictions in certain neighborhoods do not allow vegetable gardens visible from the street. I have never lived in a house with such requirements, so I had not considered the legacy of manicured outdoor space in suburban development—until I read *Levittown: Two Families, One Tycoon, and the Fight for Civil Rights in America's Legendary Suburb* by David Kushner.

Our neighborhood has never been subject to HOA (homeowners association) rules or restrictions. That is, fences can be installed and torn down, flags flown, ornamentation added, and brick walls constructed without permission from a neighborhood governing body, or HOA.

Yards must be maintained within city guidelines, which I think means that grass ought not to grow so high that critters find permanent homes within. Still, there is an unwritten code that a well-kept lawn is better than one that consists of trees, bushes, and other growing things, unless meticulously maintained.

I borrowed *Levittown* from my son's library to learn about his college studies in public policy. I knew little of this discipline and its purpose and had never considered the origin of suburban neighborhoods. As I read, I absorbed how government agencies played a role in institutionalizing racism. Their purpose was to stabilize the mortgage industry, but their policies, particularly concerning loan quality, led to discriminatory practices.

The developers of Levittown, which became a model for suburban development, marketed the uniformity of its houses within its neighborhoods. The company also promoted the misguided value of all-white neighborhoods.

Restrictive covenants in the Levittown communities that forbade nonwhite residents also dictated the frequency of grass cutting and weed removal. Just as the people inside the homes were to look alike, the exteriors were to be uniform. The modern yard was designed and maintained for appearance, not function.

The discriminatory practices discussed in the book helped me comprehend how racism became institutionalized in housing, which affects wealth accumulation. It also helped me to grasp how the notion of protecting property values can be a proxy for fear and discrimination. Those realizations were slow to crystallize but came into focus during the pandemic as I began to contemplate social injustice. Before then, though, I had felt merely inadequate, then ambivalent, at my inability to deal with outdoor space.

I felt vindicated when I learned that well-kept, weedless lawns were more marketing tools and less naturally occurring splendors. If I had researched and examined the lawn obsession, I might have discovered its origins earlier and recognized its absurdity.

Because I wasn't adept at lawn maintenance, I didn't scrutinize the costs in terms of finances, emotional labor, and time. All the watering, seeding, fertilizing, and cutting of the grass had fallen into the category of home maintenance, an inevitable expense to keep a property functioning. Also, I hadn't calculated the opportunity costs of grass lawns and the benefits of alternatives—such as vegetable gardens, fruit orchards, and flowers that could nourish my family, the community (of birds, bees, and neighbors), and me.

Instead, I admired neatly trimmed grass for its minimalistic beauty. I never considered more creative and functional uses of my yard, even as I believed a manicured lawn was unobtainable for me.

Neighborhood rules pertaining to grasses and gardens may represent ideals for some homeowners, but they do not embody the natural order of things. The manicured lawn is not a mandate from God but a human invention.

Financial services are also human inventions. They include fixed-rate mortgage loans, student loans, payday loans, credit cards, debit cards, payment apps, index funds, sales-loaded mutual funds, retirement accounts, high-deductible health care plans, FSAs (flexible savings accounts), HSAs, 401(k) plans, property and casualty insurance, and extended warranties.

Inventions are not inherently good or bad, usually, and adopting them is not uniformly wise or foolish. Several may serve my purposes in achieving financial freedom. Some may be detrimental. Many can be ignored.

57

Dig the Details

THE MORTGAGE IS AN invention. The various kinds of mortgages are also inventions, such as the thirty-year fixed-rate mortgage, the fifteen-year fixed-rate mortgage, the balloon mortgage, and the adjustable-rate mortgage. The legislation, government agencies, and businesses defining and supporting homeownership and mortgages are inventions, including federal laws relating to mortgages and homeownership, such as mortgage interest inclusion in itemized deductions and the shielding of primary homes from assets listed on FAFSA (Free Application for Federal Student Aid); the establishment of the FHA (Federal Housing Administration); and the real estate industry, including commissioned sales agents, property appraisers, and home inspectors.

You can grow wealth without studying the birth, maturity, and evolution of financial inventions, the financial services industry, and related legislation, federal and state. Such things may be considered "rocks," finer points that fascinate finance nerds. But I'll admit, on occasion, I like to pick up rocks and examine them—not real ones, mind you, as it's unlikely I could tell much from their physical characteristics given my lack of visual discernment, but financial ones—yes, please.

I've mentioned that my brain works differently than others'. One way I believe I'm different is in how I hold on to disparate facts and perspectives with the goal of one day reconciling them to each other. For example, I knew that racial discrimination persisted but didn't know precisely how institutions embedded problems into financial systems. I had an inkling that Americans worshipped property values more than is necessary or wise. Still, I didn't have firm evidence that supported my opinion or a well-defined contrarian point of view. I thought it was odd that my grandparents could remain in their home after the foreclosure. What connects the dots? I'll propose public policy.

Reading *Levittown*, contemplating the roots of injustice during the pandemic, and reflecting on my dad's stories helped me recognize how public policy affects not only our wealth-growing capacity but also what we value, sometimes without question.

During the pandemic, I reread *Levittown* to understand the sources of housing inequity better. My takeaway was that federal legislation perpetuated the untrue, hurtful idea that racial segregation and separation of social classes were essential to achieving loan quality and upholding property values.

The original intent of this legislation, however, seemed noble. Agencies were created and regulations were designed to stabilize the mortgage industry, lighten lenders' risks, and make mortgage borrowing friendlier to consumers. Changes meant that banks could safely make loans with payback over thirty years rather than five years, benefiting borrowers like my grandparents and many others during the Depression.

But to make lending profitable, there had to be safeguards for the lenders.

My curiosity prompted me to research this legislation. I learned that the federal government created the HOLC (Home Owners Loan Corporation), which extended long-term mortgages with lower interest rates to borrowers during the Depression. It also formed the FHA to guarantee loans through a mortgage insurance program. Both agencies developed ways to determine loan viability or quality, a task essential for underwriting loans, which in turn supports home affordability and the mortgage industry's stability.

There are two main aspects of loan quality: the ability of the borrower to pay back the loan according to its terms, and the worthiness of the collateral (if any) that enables the bank to recover losses should the borrower fail to repay debt.

Underwriting establishes the quality of the collateral and the customer's creditworthiness, not only for mortgages but also for other financial services. It involves reviewing applications to identify risks, setting prices relevant to these risks, and recommending approval or denial of applications, whether a loan, credit card, insurance, or other product.

Customers rated as high quality receive favorable pricing, such as lower interest rates when borrowing money.

Legislation and lending practices focused on the quality of the collateral, the real estate, measuring its current worth and likelihood to grow in value, and whether borrowers could repay their loans. Property value became integral to home buying, mortgage borrowing, and wealth building.

From what I could glean, FHA rules for evaluating risk in the 1930s and 1940s ranked specific white neighborhoods as high quality in terms of existing property values and expected value growth. At the same time, these guidelines resulted in the downgrading of mixed-race and non-white neighborhoods. Agency maps indicating neighborhood quality and, therefore, loan quality did the same. These practices became known as redlining.

Even as consumer-friendly policies emerged that helped many obtain mortgages, both through the HOLC and private lenders, institutional goals of stabilizing the industry and controlling risks conflicted with the financial aspirations of some homeowners. For example, higher interest rates charged to borrowers in neighborhoods deemed less desirable increased borrowers' costs, created higher fixed expenses relative to their incomes, and diminished opportunities to grow wealth.

Years later, credit scores were introduced to quantify creditworthiness, a borrower's ability to make payments and history in repaying loans, mortgages, credit cards, and otherwise. Individual credit scores influence the cost of financial services, including auto insurance and mortgage interest rates.

Then and now, economic conditions and institutional rules affect my finances in ways often unseen and sometimes uncontrollable.

58

Realign Values

BEFORE READING *LEVITTOWN*, RECKONING with inequities revealed in the pandemic, and reaping veggies from my garden, my general, unexamined belief regarding property values was that they represented a home's inherent worth and ought to increase over time.

In the years I did little with the yard, I fretted that inaction would diminish curb appeal and drive our house's resale price down. On occasion, I felt angst at a neighbor's slackness in exterior upkeep, worrying about its effect on my home and feeling regret at not doing better myself. Just as I believed the manicured lawn amounted to the ideal outdoor adornment, even when I did not have one, I considered property value the driving force for homeownership, even though it didn't work for me.

I appreciated the rationale for allocating an oversized percentage of income to a mortgage payment. This rationale says: Live in a dream home as a young and middle-aged adult. Itemize interest and property tax payments to reap income tax benefits. Hold wealth in home equity, which isn't included in FAFSA applications, possibly improving your children's chances of qualifying for need-based college scholarships.

When the kids are older, sell the property for a gain and avoid taxes on much of those profits.

Instead of pursuing a dream home, I avoided its high fixed expenses. I disliked depending on one asset for wealth building. Further, I lacked the visual sensitivity to choose a house and neighborhood likely to explode in market value.

After living in the rental house with the big, flat backyard for a year, my husband and I bought a house in a neighborhood close to a highway at a reasonable price. Several years later, after discovering the weakness in my visual-spatial skills, I began to focus on appearances and noticed areas that needed updates. One of our significant renovations involved the kitchen and sunroom.

We hired a contractor to oversee a project valued at close to $30,000, a significant amount compared to the home's appraised value. He replaced scuffed vinyl flooring with durable ceramic tile, ripped out pressed wood and installed natural wood cabinets, updated the 1970s-style fluorescent lighting with modern LED fixtures, put in a tile backsplash where plastic once reigned, and replaced appliances.

The January after the kitchen renovation, I noted this project on my property tax listing form, which prompted me to indicate improvements since the previous year.

A month or so later, I received a phone call from someone in my county's property appraisal division, which affected annual assessments of property taxes.

The person on the line said: "What you've listed has nothing to do with the value of your home."

I thought I had followed the rules carefully, so the intimation that I had violated one rattled me.

According to the county real estate appraiser, we had not improved the home. We had merely maintained it. He called to let me know he rejected the added value.

I was surprised filling out a form honestly had provoked suspicion.

I shared this story with friends to gain their perspectives on property appraisals. One told me he had reported a home project, and the tax value of his home increased accordingly. Another told me property appraisers gauge home value based on the outside only, period. Though I had heard of drive-by appraisals, I wondered why listing forms requested information on projects. Nevertheless, I accepted that the information provided wouldn't result in an updated property value.

In conversations with neighbors, I learned that they believed a proposed beltway near the neighborhood was suppressing property values.

At first, the mechanics of the situation seemed vague. Later, I envisioned a math-driven scenario. The neighborhood may have become less popular because of concerns about the impact of the proposed roadway. Falling popularity translated into slower turning resales and discounted pricing. Reduced prices meant lower sales comparables and valuations.

During the year we'd shopped for houses, I had tried to become attuned to potential problems that could make neighborhoods undesirable and homes less valuable. None surfaced.

But a week after closing, news headlines proclaimed a beltway would soon circle the outskirts of my city. My neighborhood would be affected. This news was not new, I learned; it had lain dormant. Realtors weren't required to mention it in their disclosures because the highway construction was stuck in the planning phase.

As a result, I concerned myself with two issues. One was the proximity of the roadway and its accompanying noise. The second was the resale value of our home.

Embedded in my concerns lived the unstated expectation of homeowners to see their homes grow in value and make money on resales. Protecting property values drove many decisions, including prices for renovations and funds poured into lawn maintenance.

Growing up in Charlotte, I watched as roads near a local park were widened in preparation for a change in traffic patterns. As a teenager, I enjoyed riding my bike in the newly expanded area, with plenty of space for both the cars and me. Later, when I returned to visit, I drove by the planned roadway and recalled the proposed construction.

Nearly thirty years after the news of the upgraded streets in Charlotte, the updates appeared in finished form. Those widened roads now carried four lanes of traffic plus a turn lane, not two as they did when I rode my bike there as a teenager. New roads connected existing streets in the area. Traffic lights were installed. All these changes combined to create new traffic patterns. I reckoned the germination of the updated roadways, seed to bloom, totaled three decades.

I never knew why roadway changes took so long to accomplish in my hometown of Charlotte. Delays near my neighborhood in Winston-Salem were due partly to budget shortfalls, more urgent priorities, and citizen concerns about environmental impact. Perhaps these hurdles were common to street construction and redesign of traffic patterns.

Whatever the reason for the delays in Charlotte and now in my current home, eventually, change arrives. For now, we've lived in our home for nearly twenty-nine years. I do not need to put together a spreadsheet to do the calculations. The beltway is coming soon.

We could have moved years ago, but we opted to stay. We like our neighbors and the neighborhood's walkability, oversized yards, and closeness to the highway.

After coming to terms with lower-than-average increases in home prices, I decided to enjoy the county appraisal and relatively low annual bills for property taxes. If the county did not want extra money from me, I was okay with that.

Several months ago, a realtor friend told me disclosures for the neighborhood are now required, nearly three decades after I first learned the news. She said property values would not change much because the positive of the highway's proximity offsets the beltway's negative.

Nevertheless, I will argue that values have changed. Mine have.

I'll affirm owning and maintaining things of value can be worthwhile. There can be beauty in an expansive home with an immaculate lawn, a three-car garage, a lake view, and an open kitchen inviting cooking and conversation.

Putting too much money into a property, however, is not a formula for my happiness. A home's significance can drift from welcoming friends, getting to know neighbors, raising children, relaxing, and enjoying walks to a relentless focus on home values and curb appeal. Perceiving the home as merely a financial asset seems not only meaningless but self-destructive and never-ending, more likely to engender a downward spiral than an ever-upward one toward contentment, compassion, gentleness, generosity, and joy.

Over time, I gained a new awareness of what I needed to thrive, aided in part by my desire to grow a garden along with relationships. Instead of anxiety over property values, I began to feel a sense of peace and gladness about my home and surroundings. This value is not about dollar signs but the connection to the community.

As I said, my values changed.

59

Choose What You Serve

More time than usual at home during the pandemic inspired schemes on ways to tend to my garden and take advantage of my yard.

As I nurtured my garden, first by prepping the soil, then sowing seeds, next looking for signs of life, monitoring and removing weeds, and gauging the ripeness of vegetables for harvest, I realized that vegetable gardening guzzles time. Certain kinds of fruit gardening, however, take minimal effort after the initial planting.

Upon making this revelation, I resolved to expand my yard's fruit-bearing capacity. Soon after, I discovered edible landscaping. This outdoor design style held the promise of turning my backyard into an asset by producing food instead of a liability requiring resources.

I found a company offering edible landscaping services and arranged for a consultation. The possibility of shame entered my mind, however, as I felt embarrassed at the weeds in my vegetable garden and the presence of a brick retaining wall in need of replacement.

I relaxed when my landscaping consultant told me a garden overgrown with weeds was commonplace. He said once the weeds become out of control, overwhelm and discouragement follow. He assured me their presence did not indicate a character defect on my part or lack of expert execution, say from the weed removal laxity, selection of poor soil, or weedy compost. I soaked up his encouragement.

His ideas reinvigorated me. He recommended a simple, chemical-free approach, requiring effort at the start and lessening in the following years. He also had a vision for my brick wall. A rebuild could double as a raised garden bed, giving me a relatively easy way to grow and maintain herbs, vine-based fruit plants, and more.

Our conversation progressed smoothly. The landscaper spoke in terms I understood. He proposed a detailed plan that meshed with my overall goals.

I liked his approach for several reasons. He acknowledged what was working well already and did not discredit me for my failures. He offered low-cost, low-maintenance ways to use an asset to produce something of value—fruit from my backyard. He explained the amount of effort I would likely expend and the level of certainty regarding results. He used language and concepts I understood and elaborated on unfamiliar ones. His methods involved respecting and harnessing nature, not consuming resources fighting it.

Getting to an agreement took some back and forth as I absorbed what he told me. He said I could create an entire orchard, filling the backyard, if I wanted. I did not. I hoped to line the yard's edges to create a border with fruit trees. He mentioned the possibility of using fruit bushes as screens, which I rejected at first, adopted, and then modified. He agreed to help me accomplish my goals with trees, bushes, and planting services.

Likewise, I have begun conversations with financial consultants with a vision but not the specifics. Once again, I felt shame at the parts of my finances not looking so good, despite my success in establishing and growing investment accounts.

In one memorable encounter, I accepted a lunch date with a financial advisor pitching his firm's services. At the exact moment I finished my meal and looked up, so did the advisor. He had ordered the same meal as I had, then matched me, bite by bite, so our forks clinked on our clean plates—*fini*—in unison.

Am I in an Alfred Hitchcock movie or at a lunch meeting?

Years after that eerie encounter, I hired this edible landscaping consultant willing to guide me, unlike the advisor who seemed intent on manipulating me.

Regarding the work for this landscaper, my focus centered on my backyard. A few years prior, my husband had arranged for the front yard to be shaped by a traditional landscaper. I may have listened to a pitch about improvements to the front, but really wanted to see what we could do about the back.

Similarly, I had been looking for help with a particular set of investment accounts, but not another portfolio that I desired to hold and manage separately. Although I may have entertained an offer to combine and control these accounts, I felt uneasy at being pressured to do so.

If my finance-related requests were impossible to fulfill or violated an advisory firm's rule, federal law, or state statute, I wanted to know, even if it conflicted with my hopes and dreams. Likewise, I appreciated hearing that Gala apples could prosper in my yard, whereas if I wanted to grow a Meyer lemon tree, I needed to bring it inside during the winter. Truthfulness helped me make sound decisions. I would be alarmed at recommendations that reinforced false beliefs and those stated as being in my best interest yet were not.

Transparency about the upfront and long-term costs also helped me make decisions. In the financial realm, there are many ways advisors make money. Some earn commissions on products they sell, such as an insurance policy or annuity. Some charge fees for completing specific tasks, such as devising a financial plan or advising on a particular topic. Others charge a percentage of assets under management (AUM) to design and manage an investment portfolio. Some work on a fee-only basis; others collect income from various methods.

A financial incentive does not produce deceit. It may, however, influence those who sell.

The mirroring advisor immersed himself in deception. After our lunch, I allowed him to send a written proposal. He and his firm proposed a "complex and sophisticated arrangement" (his words, not mine) that could protect me from a market downturn. He failed to mention this setup would trigger *short-term* capital gains taxes on long-held investments. Further, this deal would move more assets under his firm's management and generate higher AUM fees while shrinking my wealth by 35 percent immediately through taxes.

All I needed to know was I felt creeped out by this advisor's presence. Digging into the details confirmed what I suspected.

Some professionals uncover problems or identify opportunities I did not realize existed. These insights are helpful. But they should sync with my vision.

Whether my expert specializes in finance or landscaping, I want to work with someone who strives to help me achieve my goals. If I do not want an entire orchard, I should not be coerced into a tree-filled yard. I want to work with a person willing to plant a few trees.

Today, my home boasts the beginnings of a fruit orchard in its backyard and the makings of a vegetable garden alongside its south-facing side yard. The outdoors includes a deck and covered space underneath the sunroom, suitable for entertaining and relaxation.

This space nourishes me, not the other way around. Also, I don't work to preserve property values. The home and yard serve me, not the other way around.

Also, after I had the trees installed, we decided to extend the natural area of the yard to surround the trees and bushes, most of them anyway. There may be more changes in the future, as I'm experimenting with wildflowers and ground cover again. Eventually, there may be no grass to cut in the backyard.

The Unexpected Development Takeaway

LET YOUR PROPERTY, WHETHER a house or yard, serve you, not the other way around. Notice how conventional methods of growth may (or may not) benefit you and make decisions on what works best for you. Consider the worth of your home in terms of sanctuary, family, and relationships rather than increases in property values.

The Victories: Grow Confidence

60

Find Friends Growing

As I GREW IN gardening know-how, I acquired friends willing to discuss and explain garden mysteries. One patiently answered questions while visiting me for non-gardening reasons. She even spotted and identified a pepper-growing plant.

This encounter conjured fresh possibilities. Perhaps I could become the kind of person who recognized plants before the vegetables formed.

Last summer, with my garden visitor and another friend, I conversed about plants going to seed and the pH levels of soil. Neither conversation intimidated me. I defended my weed growing as part of organic gardening and received a nod of understanding.

With my newfound confidence, I envisioned converting my backyard from a traditional lawn to low-maintenance grass, fruit trees, and wildflowers. This process will take time, but with foundational knowledge, I can experiment and seek guidance to progress along the gardening learning curve.

Developing money skills also involves a learning curve.

As early as I can remember, I acted on my knowledge of money, mined experiences for personal finance lessons, gained insights into decision-making methods to be retained and discarded, and improved my understanding of wealth and its purposes. I understood that good decisions influence success but do not guarantee incredible results. I discovered sound actions are more likely to yield good outcomes when practiced consistently over multiple seasons.

Now, I also grasp why certain friends failed to convey the essence of gardening. The foundational forces of good soil, water, and sunlight may not come to mind as obvious starting points for instruction. Likewise, I may have fumbled when people asked me general questions about growing wealth—before I learned to categorize my knowledge into the essentials of saving, investing, and protecting.

I hope to emulate my friends who exude patience, honesty, and wisdom when sharing their knowledge. Not only do they commiserate about weeds, but they also share what they know in a way an earnest novice can understand and practice.

61

Crest the Learning Curve

IN THE BEGINNING, I struggled with gardening and lawn care, with their prolonged learning curves and seemingly capricious results.

Mastery was muddled because of the million rules associated with sowing, nurturing, and maintaining green things. Adhering to every gardening and lawn care truth was out of my reach. I struggled with what rules to follow because I did not know which ones mattered.

Today, I surmise a similar problem exists when people approach personal finance. There are loads of must-dos and rules of thumb, but which ones make a difference?

This question brings me back to a pandemic project—reviewing, sorting, and shredding bank statements, bills, tax records, and retirement account statements. Unboxed, this history of my financial life enlightened me.

What I found were minutiae scrutinized and managed. How many of those truly mattered?

I unearthed medical bills from the births of my children, now in their twenties.

I even found correspondence with the hospital where my older son was born after midnight. We left the hospital before dinner the next day, yet I received a bill for his overnight stay in the neonatal unit. I called and asked about the billing procedure and learned that the hospital charged parents a full day of expenses for babies present at midnight. So, what happens if the baby is never there at midnight? I pursued a response to this question to remove the charge.

There were phone calls, letters, and a long-forgotten enlistment of a mediation agency. The hospital refused to adjust that one-night charge.

Challenging bills took time. Had these battles been the best use of my time? Did they help me financially or otherwise? Could my successes help others fight similar battles?

As I review bank account, brokerage, and retirement plan statements, my pride swells as I recall my intelligent decisions. My humility surfaces as I remember many I regret. I did not know which ones would end well and which ones—not so much. Outcomes were not matched with the smartness or foolishness of financial actions. Some moves led to success, when conventional advice predicted failure, making me wonder if I was unconventionally wise or unusually lucky.

Other moves led to floundering during crises in the world and challenges at home. In the end, the managing of downturns and steadiness of effort seemed most beneficial.

My learning curve has been more winding and longer than I realized.

Arriving at the crest of a learning curve requires steady, sustained effort in receiving feedback and deciphering its meaning. Certain aspects of growing a garden and growing wealth return fast results. Whether a seed germinates or a budget covers monthly expenses becomes evident within weeks or even earlier. But whether a newly planted tree produces fruit or a recent stock purchase yields growth may take months or even years to know.

This trickling of feedback, often mixed with newly emerging and unexpected variables like a drought or economic upheaval, complicates learning. Still, knowledge accumulates over seasons.

My framework on the essentials has guided me and still informs my decisions. I started saving as a child, relearned the process as an adult, invested early with no strategy, refined my investing decision-making processes as I experienced gains and losses, and identified areas of my life requiring protection, again and again.

My theory of growing wealth by controlling spending, generating income without daily work, and protecting myself held firm. I adapted my applications of these essentials as my life and the world changed. I persist in learning, but with a better vantage point along the curve compared to where I started.

62

Enjoy a Fresh Perspective

My young adult children helped me reach a new vantage point, one that surprised me.

You may remember when I admitted I was wrong about people being either spenders or savers. Acknowledging this mistake proved easy. The difficulty arose from the process of adopting this perspective after years of believing otherwise.

This unfamiliar way of thinking began a couple of months before Hank went to college. Before then, the possibility of a spender/saver combo never entered my mind.

My son Sam is a saver, like me. He required negligible financial nurturing, no counseling about weighing the pleasure of consuming now compared to the joy of saving for later, and no admonition to set aside a certain amount of a paycheck. He saved, like I did.

Hank is a spender. No amount of effort on my part seemed to alter this trait. As a child, he pressed me to spend on Lego® toys, collectibles like Yu-Gi-Oh cards, and gaming subscriptions. As a teen, he persistently argued his way to a used car, necessary, in his mind, for transportation across town to the city's career center for AP and technical classes.

As he grew up, I heard other moms boast about a child "mini-me" who looks, sounds, and acts like them. I contended with the anti-me, the spender.

My son wanted to buy and experience many things that cost money.

Even though I labeled this child a spender, I figured he could do okay financially. He gained entrance into top engineering schools for college, so I projected that his eventual earnings would outpace his spending.

However, I wasn't prepared for his college choice. He wanted to attend an out-of-state university. I had set aside money for in-state tuition.

When I realized his decision was immovable, I started to involve him in figuring out how to cover the difference between in-state and out-of-state expenses.

Unlike Sam, he seemed uninterested in financial discussions. His high school had offered financial literacy training, which he summarized as "You go to college, you get a credit card, and then you die." I was glad he was warned about credit cards, but I wondered if that was enough. Financial lessons without immediate relevance were meaningless to him.

Many parents of college-bound students are tougher on their kids, refusing to pay any amount of college tuition or not a dime over the cost of an in-state school. Some parents are more lenient, paying for the dream school no matter what. As for me, I merely wanted his financial participation in his decision.

I considered as many options as possible. Attending community college for a couple of years and then transferring to a university didn't seem to be a wise choice, as few credits would likely transfer to his chosen degree program.

There remained three options to fund the out-of-state portion of the tuition and fees: 1) scholarships, 2) work, and 3) student loans.

Hank applied for dozens of scholarships, both while in high school and during college, all managed with a spreadsheet he designed to track application deadlines and other pertinent details. He honed his writing skills at the campus writing center. He volunteered for leadership positions and community service efforts while focusing on learning engineering principles. He visited an advisor regularly to gain insights on making himself a worthy candidate and building a more meaningful life. He spent hours improving himself to win favor from scholarship award committees.

His applying himself was part of our deal; the actual receiving of a scholarship was outside of his control. He won and received one scholarship in high school. He also won exactly one scholarship in college, which was rescinded because of his lack of financial need. Our family had the money to fund his entire education, having been fortunate with investing and having lived simply for many years.

He also applied for gobs of summer jobs, internships, and engineering-related gigs at the university. He had worked part-time in high school but was concerned about holding down a job and excelling in a challenging curriculum in college. So, he focused on summer opportunities and university jobs in the spring semester of his senior year when his course load was lighter.

Again and again, he was rejected by employers in college—with two exceptions (a youth camp and a space agency). Both positions offered learning and development, but neither paid well.

Student loans emerged as a solid, recurring, and guaranteed choice for helping to pay for college. As a parent of a dependent student and loan applicant, I completed the FAFSA to allow him to qualify. My son would then be offered a specified amount of student loans, which he could accept or reject.

Student loan debt was a concern for me and, I think, also for him.

My experiences with student loans were secondhand. My parents paid my bills. When I went to college, tuition, fees, and room and board totaled about $3,000 per year (yes, per year). Today, state universities charge ten times this amount, more for out-of-state students. I worked summers and during the school year to cover extras, like travel and dinners out.

Despite my hesitation about student loans, I appreciated that interest rates for student loans were relatively low compared to credit card interest rates. The rules allowing deferment and capitalization of interest could drive up balances, the ultimate cost of borrowing, and the length of time to payoff. I hoped that borrowing in moderation, at low interest rates, would be manageable for my son.

Before he could receive funds, my son was required by the federal agency providing student loans to complete online counseling. After he finished this session, I checked on him and noticed that he looked upset and overwhelmed, a first that I could recall.

This moment of seriousness shouldn't have surprised me. Along with my son's fierce independence, he showed unusual diligence, even as a kid. To prevent his cell phone from ringing or pinging in middle school, he disassembled it in the morning and put it back together in the afternoon. While he did buy collectibles on eBay, he also sold them there.

A couple of months after the online session, after arriving on campus, he seemed more eager than ever to analyze college costs, such as the university's meal plan, parking arrangements, bus passes, and university vs off-campus housing. Activities, whether joining a fraternity or taking a weekend trip, appeared to be weighed for costs and benefits.

Come to think of it, his brother, the saver, also entered a new, more aggressive phase in college. Saving money and outsmarting the system may have emerged as a badge of honor among their classmates. Both learned about investing from college friends. Whatever prompted it, their interest helped me when they became more money-savvy.

After college graduation and before starting his first real job, Hank held another learning session, this one in real life, with me. He asked detailed questions about investing, mainly index investing and brokerage firms. As we talked, he created a spreadsheet and devised a plan for regular savings, student loan payments, and investing.

I had fretted about his propensity for spending when he was a child. What I saw later was his ability to enjoy life, which on occasion involved parting with money. I sensed that something had shifted in him when student loan debt became real. What changed in me was realizing he could be both a spender and a saver.

63

Celebrate Mastery

PERIODICALLY, I WANDER OUTSIDE to check on my garden and yard. The more I take this step, even when I'm merely meandering, the more I notice and learn.

Although my recall of conversations and numbers goes back years, my memory of the visual is minimal. *What was our average speed the last time my friend and I rode bikes together: 17.3 mph. What scares her: getting the middle seat in an airplane, unable to stretch her legs or exit quickly if needed. What kind of car does my friend drive: I think it is white.*

My transformation to the visual has been slow but steady. Before, a mess of grass, weeds, and trees in various stages of growth and decay overtook my yard. Today, I recognize light green leaves as belonging to tomato plants, yellow blooms indicating a forthcoming zucchini, and vine-like shoots with heart-shaped leaves as weeds.

I began this yard development process with hopelessness, the sole encouragement coming from a self-made gardening instructor I found on the internet.

Now, I feel amazed at what I have mastered, even as I remain a student. I can visualize the root system of an insidious wildflower with beautiful purple blooms in the spring and hideous leaves in the summer. I recognize plants and know what to expect beyond buds in the spring and leaves in the fall.

Surprises sneak in, like the cilantro that appeared a full year after I sowed its seeds or the peppers that started as sweet round balls but never matured. I accept the gifts and the disappointments.

Today, I approach my finances mostly with confidence.

I review my accounts on a regular, though not regimented, basis. I look at my checking account to notice what transactions have cleared. I study my credit card statements for unusual charges. I check on investment balances to see what stocks have grown in value and which ones have languished. Before I look, I tend to know what to expect based on market happenings and recent contributions to my accounts.

Separately, I consider strategy and day-to-day tactics. Results from real-life activities sharpen my understanding of theory, which in turn helps me plot next steps.

I started by learning and practicing the essentials. Knowledge and understanding accumulated and then compounded.

The Victories Takeaway

Success builds upon itself, just as pennies compound to dollars. As you progress in acumen, you can have more productive conversations, learn more, and advance in knowledge and accomplishments. Celebrate your successes even as you continue to learn.

Epilogue

Stay Focused on Purpose

LAST SUMMER, IN ADDITION to tending my garden and starting a fruit orchard, I participated in a virtual competition called "Take the Lake Challenge." To complete the challenge, participants tracked and reported their runs, walks, bike rides, and swims from July 1 to September 30 with the aim of completing five hundred and twenty miles, the length of the perimeter of a nearby lake. The benefits were twofold: staying active during the pandemic and supporting the challenge's sponsor in serving the community through the entry fee.

The challenge offered categories for individuals as well as two-, three-, four-, and five-person teams. I entered as part of a two-person team consisting of my husband and me. As participants entered workout mileages, individual and team results were tallied and ranked by miles completed on the event's website. After reaching the goal, participants received commemorative T-shirts, socks, and medals. Many, including me, kept logging miles even after reaching this milestone.

In September, with a few weeks left in the challenge, I ranked second place for individual mileage within the two-person category.

This standing was unintentional—in the beginning, anyway. I spent the summer doing what I enjoyed, riding bikes with my friends, walking a bit, and running some. I recorded my miles on the race's website and then found myself in a competition. I analyzed the patterns of the person in first place as well as the one in third place and decided they may have upped their mileage game this summer. But then, so did I.

I debated whether to abandon all other plans in order to log a significant number of miles and reign as champion in this obscure virtual race. Then I wondered if what started as a healthy distraction held the seeds for becoming a destructive one.

For the past forty years, I had avoided competing with anyone but myself, though I remained aware of the relevant stats of others around me.

Before I run a race, I analyze the previous finish times of all the women in my age group. I plan pacing for every stretch of the route from the adrenaline-fueled start through the downhills, false flats, and turns to the finish line. However, my goal is always to achieve a particular time, not best a specific person.

I will admit I adopted this stance only after seeing a look of anguish on the face of a friend and swimming competitor. I had beaten her in a summer league swim competition, obscure like this summer challenge but seemingly monumental in the moment.

What disturbed me was that I had *wanted* her to look this way, distressed at her defeat.

I surmised she hadn't expected me to win. She had dominated me for years, with her long reach and body length extending a foot past mine. I improved by swimming year-round. She swam through all the seasons like me, but sometimes finished her laps by walking on the pool floor, reducing the effectiveness of her workouts. I persisted until my hands or flip-turned feet touched the pool wall.

When I noticed my standing in the summer challenge, I may have felt the need to prove how I had overcome an unlevel playing field, like I had when I was a teenager with my swimming buddy. I ranked as one of the older entrants and wanted to make sixty-something females like me proud.

As a kid, I enjoyed swimming, riding my bike, and walking a mile to the 7-Eleven for a ten-cent ICEE® with a friend (eleven cents with tax). I was a regular-sized child and as strong as others—until adolescence when the boys could suddenly slam a tennis ball my way fiercer than a year before, and everyone became taller, except me.

Reluctantly but decidedly, I accepted how my slow, deliberate thinking and lack of hand-eye coordination detracted from my abilities on ballfields. But I persisted in other realms—swimming, running, and cycling—despite my height and reach limitations.

What hurt the most was being overlooked, yes, literally and figuratively, by coaches who ogled the tall kids and the naturals who didn't require actual coaching to excel. There were notable exceptions, including a high school coach who taught me how to develop distance running abilities and congratulated me on earning an athletic letter in track as a senior (an accomplishment since as a sophomore I couldn't run a quarter mile without incurring side stitches).

I gravitated toward sports for a few reasons. I genuinely liked them, for starters. Plus, these activities allowed me to use numbers to analyze my performance, whether distance, elevation gain, speed, or something else. Perhaps most important, I tended to make friends more readily in these realms. The pattern persists today, as my social life equates closely with my active life.

When I reflect more on this playing field, I recognize not only my disadvantages but also my advantages, which I worked hard to capitalize on. For example, my first memory of swimming was simply doing it; I don't recall ever learning how to hold my breath and glide underwater.

As a kid growing up in the 1960s and 1970s in suburban Charlotte, I gained basic fitness by walking and riding my bike as my primary forms of transportation—with little parental or neighborly interference. Kids and teens today sometimes get harassed, or their parents do, for the simple act of walking to and from school, as if it's truancy or rebellion.

From a young age, I learned what to do to improve my speed, endurance, and love of sport, starting with swim practice at age six. There were times when I floundered but just as often when I found friends to accompany me and teach me what I needed to know. There was the high school coach who suggested a pattern of running and walking to build endurance, years before the run-walk became popular, the friend who suggested a sports watch to help me break the ten-minute-per-mile barrier as a runner in my fifties, and the cycling mentor who showed me how to navigate clipped-in shoes and roads with car traffic.

Now I view the approaches taken by my coaches and buddies as similar to the one offered by my gardening instructor. They were knowledgeable and discerning, giving me essential yet crucial guidance on getting started and making progress. They never shamed me for asking a question or not knowing how to do something.

I also grasp that playing fields are often unlevel for unobvious reasons. Sure, an inheritance creates an advantage in accumulating wealth, as does having a parent who runs a family farm in gardening. But there are also affinities and innate strengths that influence success in ways we may not fathom until we examine our capabilities. Further, one person may accelerate along a learning curve, whereas another lingers for long periods, even though both progress.

Personal advantages and giftedness do not negate the importance of diligence and hard work. I stand firm that my win in the swimming race resulted partly from my refusal to walk on the pool floor in practice! However, my natural talents may have played a role in my placing first, along with my certainty that swim practice would give me the rewards I sought.

Likewise, compounding pennies and dollars made sense to me from the start, whereas nurturing vegetables seemed a mysterious happening with chaotic rules. Before my lessons, industriousness at gardening didn't get me anywhere except perhaps increasingly exasperated at a string of confusing failures. My gardening teacher reversed this trajectory, establishing the essentials from which further experience and learning expanded.

I wonder if others feel about money as I have felt about gardening. Sure, some persist in their spendthrift ways on purpose, but many may not have the foundational knowledge to assure their hard work yields a return. Mix in faux advisors and financial institutions that place their interests above their customers, and the results are disastrous.

About that swim race, again, I planned to win, yet I failed to consider my friend's dejection. I merely wanted to best her in the race.

Then I saw how losing to me caused her anguish.

After seeing the look on her face, I resolved never to strategize to beat anyone, ever again, friend or not. I adopted setting personal goals, never to defeat a friend or pass someone I identified as my competition in a race. If I happened to swim, run, or move faster than a friend or fellow racer, it would depend on her perspective whether she felt sad.

I never wavered from this attitude until the summer of the lake competition.

I reminded myself that I had entered the virtual challenge for two reasons: 1) to motivate myself and my husband to stay active during the pandemic, and 2) to give money to the race sponsor's cause, an outreach of a church distributing food and clothing to people in a different neighborhood of my city.

A couple of years ago, I read an admonition to would-be philanthropists that made this project attractive. The source seems fuzzy now, but I recall the provocative statement: Giving to others who look like me is not generous or charitable. It merely protects the status quo.

That made me pause. I stored it away for reflection. Later, when the roots of injustice were exposed to me during the pandemic, the statement about giving made sense. I did not agree wholeheartedly, yet I understood the author's point. I felt excited to enjoy a virtual challenge while helping people who did not look like me.

Remembering my friend's look, I stepped away from my desire to achieve the top ranking in my fifty-person division. I set a goal maximum of fifteen hundred miles and stopped trying to one-up my challenge buddies. (I finished in second place, with over thirteen hundred miles.)

I also realized the wisdom of applying this approach to my finances. My ambition is not to stand on the podium of status attained through spending or wealth accumulation. I aim to achieve my goals for growth—whether as an investor, gardener, or athlete—as I pursue meaningful challenges, peace of mind, and freedom for my family, my community, and me.

Acknowledgments

Thank you to my family who taught, supported, and challenged me: my dad, Hall Starnes, who gave me quick yet meaningful lessons about money; my mom, Jenny Starnes, who urged me to save for and enjoy rainy days; my husband, Tim, who encouraged me in all aspects of learning, writing, and growing; my sons, Sam and Hank, who gave live demos of different learning and money styles; and my daughter-in-law, Lindsey, who loves us anyway and is ever encouraging us to be our best, authentic selves.

Thank you to the dozens of people who read my words in rough and polished form and offered their reactions so I could see my words through your eyes and refine my written expressions. Thank you to my inner circle of writers, a.k.a. the Writer's Salon, who guided me while sharing their stories and progress to published authorship, particularly Kira Higgs, Terri Tomoff, Katy Dalgleish, Kym Dakin, Lynn Carnes, and Geoff Saab.

Thank you to all the people with whom I've interacted in learning to garden, grow wealth, master anything new, and write and publish a book. Thank you for helping me to appreciate and share my God-given talents.

Notes

Chapter 24

https://www.cdc.gov/botulism/surv/2018/index.html.

Chapter 30 and Chapter 32

Dorsey, Pat. *The Five Rules for Successful Stock Investing: Morningstar's Guide to Building Wealth and Winning in the Market.* Wiley, 2003.

Graham, Benjamin. Jason Zweig. Warren E. Buffett (Collaborator). *The Intelligent Investor: The Definitive Book on Value Investing (Revised Edition).* New York. HarperCollins Publishers, 2006.

Chapter 43

Koscielniak, Bruce. *Bear and Bunny Grow Tomatoes.* Knopf Books for Young Readers, 1993.

Chapter 56

Kushner, David. *Levittown: Two Families, One Tycoon, and the Fight for Civil Rights in America's Legendary Suburb*. Walker Books, 2009.

Suggested Reading

Burrough, Bryan. John Helyar. *Barbarians at the Gate: The Fall of RJR Nabisco.* Harper & Row, 1989.

Fishback, Price. Jonathan Rose. Kenneth Snowden. *Well Worth Saving: How the New Deal Safeguarded Home Ownership (National Bureau of Economic Research Series on Long-Term Factors in Economic Development).* The University of Chicago Press, 2013.

Wineka, Mark, and Jason Lesley. *Lion's Share: How Three Small-Town Grocers Created America's Fastest-Growing Supermarket Chain and Made Millionaires of Scores of Their North Carolina Friends and Neighbors.* Asheboro, NC. Down Home Press, 1991.

Spreadsheet Examples

Chapter 12: Fixed, Variable, and Discretionary Budgeting Framework.

Chapter 30: Sequence-of-Returns Risk.

Chapters 47 and 49: Compound Growth and Time Value of Money.

Chapter 50: Cash Flow Example.

Find these spreadsheet examples here:

https://www.julierains.com/resources

Index

The Intelligent Investor, 124

About the Author

JULIE RAINS IS A writer and investor. She has served as a financial analyst and accountant for Fortune 500 corporations and a freelance writer for individual clients and media companies. Consistently, her work has involved analyzing financial information and crafting narratives to make sense of the math.

She and her husband, Tim, raised two sons, now grown. They live in North Carolina, where she attempts to grow things, rides her bike, and occasionally organizes group hikes.

Made in the USA
Monee, IL
04 November 2026

67384729R00154